NEED to KNOW

AQA A-LEVEL ECONOMICS

Key facts at your fingertips

David Horner
Steve Stoddard

HODDER
EDUCATION
AN HACHETTE UK COMPANY

Hachette UK's policy is to use papers that are natural, renewable and recyclable products and made from wood grown in sustainable forests. The logging and manufacturing processes are expected to conform to the environmental regulations of the country of origin.

Orders: please contact Bookpoint Ltd, 130 Park Drive, Milton Park, Abingdon, Oxon OX14 4SE. Telephone: (44) 01235 827827. Fax: (44) 01235 400401. Email: education@bookpoint.co.uk

Lines are open from 9 a.m. to 5 p.m., Monday to Saturday, with a 24-hour message answering service. You can also order through our website: www.hoddereducation.co.uk

ISBN: 978 1 5104 2849 2

First published in 2018 by
Hodder Education,
An Hachette UK Company
Carmelite House
50 Victoria Embankment
London EC4Y 0DZ

Impression number   10 9 8 7 6 5 4 3 2 1

Year   2022 2021 2020 2019 2018

Typeset in India by Aptara Inc.

Printed in Spain

A catalogue record for this title is available from the British Library.

MIX
Paper from
responsible sources
FSC™ C104740

Contents

Getting the most from this book

This *Need to Know* guide is designed to help you throughout your course as a companion to your learning and a revision aid in the months or weeks leading up to the final exams.

The following features in each section will help you get the most from the book.

You need to know

Each topic begins with a list summarising what you 'need to know' in this topic for the exam.

Exam tip

Key knowledge you need to demonstrate in the exam, tips on exam technique, common misconceptions to avoid and important things to remember.

Key terms

Definitions of highlighted terms in the text to make sure you know the essential terminology for your subject.

Do you know?

Questions at the end of each topic to test you on some of its key points. Check your answers here: www.hoddereducation.co.uk/needtoknow/answers

Synoptic links

Reminders of how knowledge and skills from different topics in your A-level relate to one another.

End of section questions

Questions at the end of each main section of the book to test your knowledge of the specification area covered. Check your answers here: www.hoddereducation.co.uk/needtoknow/answers

1 Individuals, firms, markets and market failure

1.1 Economic methodology and the economic problem

You need to know

- the methodology used by economists
- the nature and purpose of economic activity
- the key economic resources
- the economic problem of scarcity and why choices must be made in allocating economic resources

Economic methodology

Economics:

- studies how the world's scarce resources are allocated to competing uses to satisfy society's wants
- is a social science
- attempts to use scientific methodology for observing human behaviour and then makes predictions

Exam tip

A positive statement need not necessarily be factually true. It simply needs to be capable of being tested to be declared true or false.

Key terms

Positive economic statement An objective statement that can be tested against the facts to be declared either true or false.

Normative economic statement A subjective opinion, or value judgement that cannot be declared either true or false.

Key terms

Need Something that humans need to survive, e.g. food, shelter and warmth.

Want Something that people feel improves their standard of living but is not required for survival, e.g. a new car.

The nature and purpose of economic activity

- The main purpose of economic activity is to satisfy society's **needs** and **wants**.
- **Economic welfare** is the standard of living or general well-being of individuals in society.

Economic resources

Factor of production	Definition	Example
Capital	Man-made physical equipment used to make other goods and services	Machinery and computer equipment
Enterprise	Individuals who take a business risk in combining the other three factors of production in order to produce a good or service	Jeff Bezos, Richard Branson, James Dyson
Land	All naturally occurring resources	Minerals, the sea, fertile land and the environment
Labour	People involved in production, sometimes referred to as human capital	Teacher, accountant, farmer

Scarcity, choice and the allocation of resources

- Scarcity means that economic resources are limited relative to society's wants.
- Choices are made when allocating resources.
- We must consider the three fundamental economic questions:
  - ☐ **What** to produce and in what quantities?
  - ☐ **How** should goods and services be produced?
  - ☐ **To whom** should goods and services be allocated?

Economic systems

- **Free market** or **capitalist economy**: decisions are made solely by the interactions of consumers and firms, with no government intervention.
- **Command** or **centrally planned economy**: decisions are made solely by governments.

Opportunity cost, economic goods and free goods

Production possibility diagrams

Figure 1 shows a **production possibility curve** (PPC).

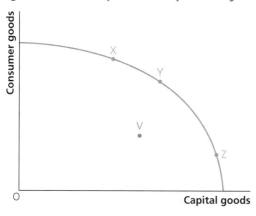

Figure 1 A production possibility curve

- Any point on the production possibility curve, e.g. X, Y or Z, means all factors of production are fully employed.
- An economy operating at point V is operating inefficiently, with unused resources, e.g. unemployed labour.

Shifts of the PPC

Factors causing an outward shift of the PPC	Factors causing an inward shift of the PPC
■ Technological improvements ■ Discovery of new resources, e.g. oil and gas ■ Improvements in education and training ■ Demographic changes, e.g. increases in immigration or an increased retirement age	■ Natural disasters, e.g. earthquakes or floods ■ Wars ■ Global warming/climate change, leading to loss of farmland, rising sea levels and extreme weather ■ A prolonged recession, which may lead to permanent loss of productive capacity

Using a PPC diagram to show opportunity cost

The PPC in Figure 2 shows the concept of opportunity cost. Moving from point A to point B involves giving up LR consumer goods to gain MS capital goods.

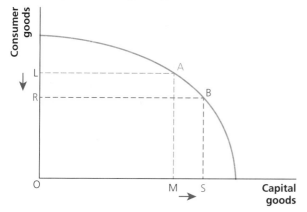

Figure 2 The production possibility curve and opportunity cost

> **Key term**
>
> **Production possibility curve (PPC)** A diagram that shows the maximum possible output combinations of two goods in an economy, assuming full employment of efficient resources.

> **Exam tip**
>
> Production possibility diagrams may also be referred to as **production possibility frontiers** (PPFs) and **production possibility boundaries** (PPBs).

> **Exam tip**
>
> Do not confuse an increased utilisation of factors of production with economic growth. An increased utilisation of factors of production moves the economy to a point closer to the PPC, whereas economic growth leads to an outward shift of the PPC.

Using a PPC diagram to show economic growth

Key term

Economic growth An increase in the productive capacity of an economy over time.

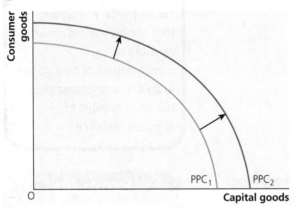

Figure 3 The production possibility curve and economic growth

An improvement in technology or any of the factors that lead to an outward shift of the PPC, as shown in Figure 3, means that there has been an increase in the productive capacity of the economy.

Synoptic link

PPC diagrams can be used to model microeconomic situations, at the level of the individual and the firm, as well as macroeconomic situations affecting the economy as a whole.

Economic efficiency and production possibility diagrams

Key terms

Productive efficiency When maximum output is produced from the available factors of production and when it is not possible to produce more of one good or service without producing less of another.

Allocative efficiency When an economy's factors of production are used to produce the combination of goods and services that maximises society's welfare.

- The concepts of **productive efficiency** and productive inefficiency are shown in Figure 4.
- The **allocatively efficient** point on the PPC is the one that best reflects society's preferences for particular goods and services.

Exam tip

Learn how to draw PPC diagrams to illustrate efficiency, scarcity, choice and opportunity cost at the microeconomic level, as well as economic growth, full employment and unemployment at a macroeconomic level.

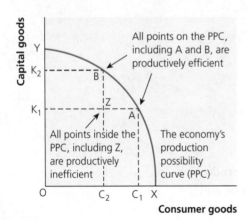

Figure 4 Productive efficiency and the PPC

Do you know?

1 Explain why economics is referred to as a social science.
2 State and give examples of each of the four factors of production.
3 Explain the difference between positive and normative economic statements.
4 State and explain the basic economic problem.
5 Sketch PPC diagrams to show the following: productive efficiency, opportunity cost, economic growth.

1.2 Individual economic decision making

You need to know

- traditional and modern views of consumer behaviour
- the meaning and consequences of imperfect information
- aspects of behavioural economic theory
- how behavioural economics can be applied to economic policy

Key terms

Utility The amount of satisfaction or benefit that a consumer gains from consuming a good or service.

Rational consumer An assumption of traditional economic theory that consumers act in such a way as always to maximise satisfaction, or utility, when they spend money on goods and services.

Marginal utility The satisfaction gained from consuming an additional unit of a good or service.

Diminishing marginal utility As individuals consume more units of a good or service, the additional units give successively smaller increases in total satisfaction.

Consumer behaviour

Utility theory

Traditional, neoclassical economic theory assumes consumers always act rationally, seeking to maximise satisfaction for every pound spent.

Diminishing marginal utility

- **Diminishing marginal utility** is a way of deriving an individual's downward-sloping demand curve for a good or service, as shown in Figure 5.
- As marginal utility declines, the price the consumer is willing to pay for additional units decreases.

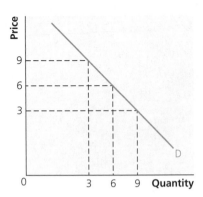

Figure 5 Diminishing marginal utility and the individual demand curve

Imperfect information

- Behavioural economics recognises that humans will not always make rational decisions.
- This makes it difficult for economic agents to make rational decisions and is a potential source of market failure.

Sources of imperfect information

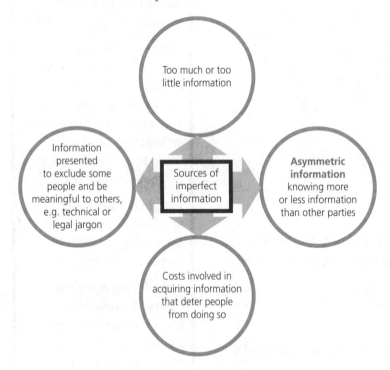

Asymmetric information

- When one party (usually the seller) has more/superior information than another (usually the buyer).
- Leads to an imbalance of power: one party can exploit the other, resulting in market failure.
- Leads to a lack of trust between agents, so a mutually beneficial exchange does not occur.

Aspects of behavioural economic theory

Key terms

Bounded rationality When people try to behave rationally but cannot, due to information being incomplete, unreliable or complex.

Bounded self-control When individuals have good intentions but lack the self-discipline to see them through, e.g. saving for the future.

Rules of thumb Shortcuts in thinking that individuals use to make decisions in order to save time and effort.

Anchoring The tendency of individuals to rely on particular pieces of information when making choices between different goods and services, e.g. choosing between car insurance companies.

Availability bias When people make judgements about the probability of events by recalling recent instances.

Social norms The influence of others on individual decision-making, e.g. encouraging passengers to put pressure on drivers not to drive under the influence of alcohol.

Altruism and fairness When people are motivated to 'do the right thing', e.g. giving to charity or doing voluntary work.

Behavioural economics and economic policy

Key terms

Choice architecture Influencing consumer choices by the way the choices are presented in order to achieve desired outcomes, e.g. organ donation.

Framing Influencing consumer choices by the way words and numbers are used, e.g. presenting life insurance premium payments as 'less than £3 per day' sounds more palatable than '£1,000 per year'.

Nudges Influencing consumer behaviour via the use of gentle suggestions and positive reinforcement, e.g. the 'five-a-day' campaign to encourage greater consumption of fruit and vegetables.

Default choice Influencing consumer behaviour by setting socially desirable choices as default options.

Key terms

Mandated choice Where people are legally required to make a particular choice, e.g. in many countries people are required to make a decision about organ donation as part of their driving licence or passport application.

Restricted choice Giving consumers a limited number of options when making a choice, e.g. with savings or pensions, a limited number of options may be better.

Do you know?

1 Explain what is meant by diminishing marginal utility.
2 State three sources of imperfect information.
3 Explain the terms 'bounded rationality' and 'anchoring'.
4 Explain how nudges could be used to influence consumers to make better choices in relation to a healthy lifestyle.

1.3 Price determination in a competitive market

You need to know

- the meaning of a competitive market
- the determinants of the demand for goods and services
- price, income and cross elasticities of demand
- the determinants of the supply of goods and services
- price elasticity of supply
- the determination of equilibrium market prices
- the interrelationship between markets

The meaning of a competitive market

- A **market** does not have to occur in a physical location.
- There are a large number of potential buyers and sellers, all individually powerless to influence the ruling market price.
- This price, known as the **equilibrium price**, is determined by the interaction of market demand and market supply.

Determinants of the demand for goods and services

- **Demand** is the quantity of a good or service that consumers are willing and able to buy at given prices in a particular time period.
- Economists are concerned with **effective demand**.

The law of demand and the shape of the market demand curve

- The 'law' of demand states that as the price of a good or service falls, the quantity demanded increases.
- This inverse relationship between the price and quantity demanded of a good or service is shown in Figure 6.
- An increase in the quantity demanded resulting from a fall in price is known as an extension of demand, whereas a fall in quantity demanded resulting from an increase in price is known as a contraction of demand.

Key terms

Market A situation in which buyers and sellers come together to engage in trade.

Competitive market A situation where there are a large potential number of buyers and sellers with abundant information about the market.

Equilibrium price The price at which the planned demand of consumers equals the planned supply of firms.

Effective demand Consumers' desire to buy a good, backed up by the ability to pay.

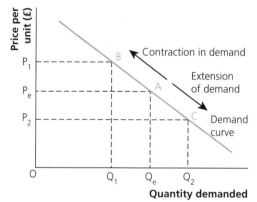

Figure 6 Movements along a demand curve

Factors that shift a demand curve

- real disposable incomes
- tastes and preferences (fashions)
- population
- prices of **substitute** products
- prices of **complementary** products

If any of these **conditions of demand** change, the demand curve for the good or service will change.

This leads to a rightward or leftward shift of the demand curve, as shown in Figure 7.

- A rightward shift is an increase in demand, whereas a leftward shift is a decrease in demand.

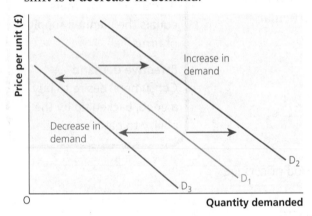

Figure 7 **Shifts of the demand curve**

Key terms

Substitute A good which may be consumed as an alternative to another good.

Complement A good which tends to be consumed together with another good.

Conditions of demand Factors other than the price of the good that lead to a change in position of the demand curve.

Price elasticity of demand The responsiveness of the quantity demanded of a good or service to a change in price.

Price, income and cross elasticities of demand

Price elasticity of demand

- The formula for **price elasticity of demand** (PED) is as follows:

$$PED = \frac{\text{percentage change in quantity demanded}}{\text{percentage change in price}}$$

- The value for price elasticity of demand is usually negative because of the assumed inverse relationship between price and quantity demanded.
- We tend to ignore the minus sign in any calculation.

Exam tip

Memorise the percentage change formula:

$$\text{percentage change} = \frac{\text{change}}{\text{original value}} \times 100$$

Key values and explanations

Term	Explanation	Example
Price inelastic demand	When demand for a product is price inelastic, the value of PED is between 0 and 1, ignoring the minus sign	A 50% increase in the price of petrol leads to a 10% fall in quantity demanded: $$PED = \frac{-10}{+50} = -0.2$$
Price elastic demand	When demand for a product is price elastic, the value of PED is greater than 1, ignoring the minus sign.	A 10% reduction in the price of cars leads to a 15% increase in quantity demanded: $$PED = \frac{+15}{-10} = -1.5$$
Unitary elastic demand	When demand is unitary elastic, the value of PED is exactly 1, ignoring the minus sign. The demand curve is a rectangular hyperbola	A 20% increase in the price of a mobile phone leads to a 20% decrease in quantity demanded: $$PED = \frac{-20}{+20} = -1.0$$
Perfectly inelastic demand	When demand for a product is perfectly price inelastic, the value of PED is 0. The demand curve will be vertical	A 10% increase in the price of a carton of milk leads to no change in quantity demanded: $$PED = \frac{0}{+10} = 0.0$$
Perfectly elastic demand	When demand is perfectly elastic, the value of PED is infinity. The demand curve will be horizontal	An extremely small increase in the price of a product leads to the quantity demanded falling to zero

Price elasticity of demand and total revenue

The PED of a product determines what happens to consumer spending (and therefore total revenue) following a price change.

- If demand is price elastic, a reduction in price leads to an increase in total revenue.
- If demand is price inelastic, a reduction in price leads to a decrease in total revenue.
- If demand is price elastic, a price increase leads to a reduction in total revenue.
- If demand is price inelastic, a price increase leads to an increase in total revenue.

Determinants of price elasticity of demand

- availability of close substitutes
- percentage of income spent on the product
- nature of the product
- time period
- broad or specific market definition

Income elasticity of demand

The formula for **income elasticity of demand** (YED) is:

$$\text{YED} = \frac{\text{percentage change in quantity demanded}}{\text{percentage change in real income}}$$

Key values

- For YED the sign is important.
- If the value is positive, i.e. greater than 0, the product is a normal good. This means a rise in income will lead to an increase in demand.
- If the value is negative, i.e. less than 0, the product is an inferior good. This means a rise in income will lead to a fall in demand.

> **Key term**
>
> **Income elasticity of demand** The responsiveness of demand of a good to a change in consumers' real income.

Term	Explanation	Example
Income elastic	When demand for a product is income elastic, the value of YED is greater than +1 Income elastic products are often referred to as luxury goods	Example: a 10% increase in real income leads to a 20% increase in demand for foreign holidays: $\text{YED} = \dfrac{+20}{+10} = +2.0$
Income inelastic	When demand for a product is income inelastic, the value of YED is between 0 and +1 Income inelastic products are often referred to as basic goods or necessities	Example: a 10% increase in real income leads to a 2% increase in demand for cartons of milk: $\text{YED} = \dfrac{+2}{+10} = +0.2$
Negative income elastic	When demand for a product is negative income elastic, the value of YED is negative, i.e. less than 0 Negative income elastic products are referred to as inferior goods	Example: a 20% increase in real income leads to a 10% fall in demand for a supermarket's value brand of baked beans: $\text{YED} = \dfrac{-10}{+20} = -0.5$

Cross elasticity of demand

The formula for **cross elasticity of demand** (XED) is:

$$\text{XED} = \frac{\text{percentage change in quantity demanded of product A}}{\text{percentage change in price of product B}}$$

Key values

- For XED the sign is important.
- A positive value means products A and B are substitutes, i.e. a rise in the price of product B leads to an increase in demand for product A.
- A negative value means products A and B are complements, i.e. a rise in price of product B leads to a fall in the demand for product A.
- Example: a 20% increase in the price of cod leads to a 10% fall in the demand for chips.

> **Key terms**
>
> **Cross elasticity of demand** The responsiveness of the demand for a product following a change in price of another product.
>
> **Supply** The quantity of a good or service that firms plan to sell at given prices in a particular time period.

$$XED = \frac{-10}{+20} = -0.5$$

The two products are therefore complements.

Determinants of the supply of goods and services

The law of supply

- The law of supply states that as price increases the quantity supplied will increase.
- This positive relationship is shown in Figure 8.

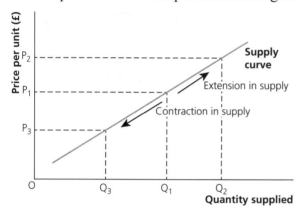

Figure 8 Movements along a supply curve

- Firms are assumed to want to maximise their profits; a higher price is an incentive to increase production.
- A change in price will lead to a movement along an existing supply curve.
- An increase in price leads to an increase in quantity supplied — an extension of supply.
- A decrease in price leads to a decrease in quantity supplied — a contraction in supply.

Factors that shift a supply curve

- production costs
- productivity of labour
- taxes on businesses
- production subsidies
- technology

If any of these **conditions of supply** change, the supply curve for the good or service will change.

This leads either to a rightward or leftward shift of the supply curve, as shown in Figure 9.

- A rightward shift is an increase in supply.
- A leftward shift is a decrease in supply.

Key term

Conditions of supply Factors other than the price of the good that lead to a change in position of the supply curve.

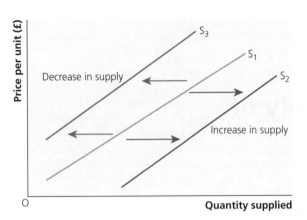

Figure 9 Shifts of a supply curve

Price elasticity of supply

The formula for **price elasticity of supply** (PES) is:

$$PES = \frac{percentage\ change\ in\ quantity\ supplied}{percentage\ change\ in\ price}$$

Key values

Price elasticity of supply always has a positive value because of the positive relationship between price and quantity supplied.

> **Key term**
>
> **Price elasticity of supply**
> The responsiveness of the quantity supplied of a good or service to a change in price.

Term	Explanation	Example
Price inelastic supply	When the supply of a product is price inelastic, the value of PES is between 0 and 1. The supply curve will be relatively steep	Example: a 20% increase in the price of barley leads to a 5% increase in quantity supplied: $PES = \frac{+5}{+20} = +0.25$
Price elastic supply	When the supply of a product is price elastic, the value of PES is greater than 1. The supply curve will be relatively shallow	Example: a 5% fall in the price of carpets leads to a 10% fall in quantity supplied: $PES = \frac{-10}{-5} = +2.0$
Unitary elastic supply	When the supply of a product is unitary elastic, the value of PES is exactly 1. The supply curve is a straight line drawn through the origin	Example: a 15% increase in the price of table salt leads to a 15% increase in quantity supplied: $PES = \frac{+15}{+15} = +1.0$
Perfectly inelastic supply	When the supply of a product is perfectly inelastic, the value of PES is zero. The supply curve is vertical	Example: a 5% increase in the price of copper leads to zero increase in the quantity supplied: $PES = \frac{0}{+5} = 0$
Perfectly elastic supply	When the supply of a product is perfectly elastic, the value of PES is infinity. The supply curve is horizontal	Example: a 2% increase in the price of a downloadable song leads to an infinitely large increase in quantity supplied

Determinants of price elasticity of supply

- time taken to expand supply
- size of spare capacity
- available stocks
- ease of switching production

Determination of equilibrium market prices

- Equilibrium market price and quantity are determined by the interaction of the market demand and supply curves for a particular good or service, as shown in Figure 10.
- When quantity demanded equals quantity supplied in a market for a particular product, the market is in equilibrium.

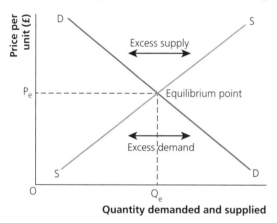

Figure 10 Equilibrium price and quantity

Market disequilibrium occurs when quantity demanded does not equal quantity supplied.

- If price is above market equilibrium price (P_e), there is **excess supply**.
- If price is below market equilibrium price (P_e), there is **excess demand**.
- Eventually, **market forces** lead to excess supply or excess demand being resolved.

Changes in equilibrium price

These may be caused by either a shift of the demand curve or a shift of the supply curve (resulting from a change in the conditions of demand or supply).

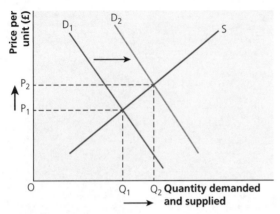

Figure 11 An increase in demand

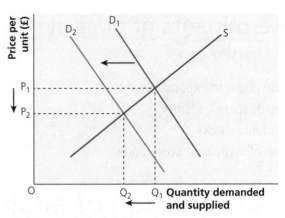

Figure 12 A decrease in demand

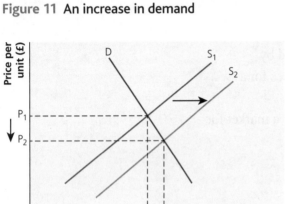

Figure 13 An increase in supply

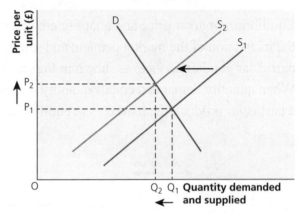

Figure 14 A decrease in supply

Term	Explanation	Example
Increase in demand	This would lead to an increase in equilibrium price and quantity as shown in Figure 11	Following an increase in real incomes, the demand curve of a normal good, such as going to the cinema, would shift rightwards
Decrease in demand	This will lead to a decrease in equilibrium price and quantity as shown in Figure 12	Following a fall in real incomes, the demand curve of a normal good would shift leftwards
Increase in supply	This will lead to a decrease in equilibrium price and an increase in quantity as shown in Figure 13	Following a good harvest, the supply curve of coffee would shift rightwards
Decrease in supply	This will lead to an increase in equilibrium price and a decrease in quantity as shown in Figure 14	Following a poor harvest, the supply curve of wheat would shift leftwards

The interrelationship between markets

Shifts of demand and supply curves arise not only from changes in market conditions for the product in question, but also from changes in associated markets.

Joint demand

- Also known as complementary goods, i.e. goods that tend to be demanded together such as cars and fuel, e.g. as demand for cars increases, demand for fuel increases.
- The opposite effect to substitutes (competing demand), e.g. as demand for cars increases, demand for public transport decreases.

Joint supply

- When production of one good also leads to production of another good, e.g. production of beef and leather, both arising from cattle farming.

Composite demand

- When a good is demanded for more than one distinct use.
- An increase in demand for one distinct use reduces the supply available for other uses.

Derived demand

- When a particular good or factor of production is necessary for provision of another good or service, e.g. an increase in demand for healthcare is likely to lead to an increase in demand for doctors.

> ## Key terms
>
> **Joint demand** Goods which tend to be demanded together, i.e. complementary goods.
>
> **Joint supply** When the production of one good leads to the production of another good.
>
> **Composite demand** When a good is demanded for more than one distinct use.
>
> **Derived demand** When a particular good or factor of production is necessary for the provision of another good or service.

Do you know?

1 State three determinants of demand.
2 State three determinants of price elasticity of demand.
3 Explain how price elasticity of demand influences total revenue.
4 State three determinants of supply.
5 State three determinants of price elasticity of supply.

1.4 Production, costs and revenue

You need to know

- production and productivity
- specialisation, division of labour and exchange
- costs of production
- the law of diminishing returns and returns to scale
- costs of production in the long run
- economies and diseconomies of scale
- average revenue, total revenue and profit
- market structure and marginal and average revenue
- technological change

Figure 15 shows the building blocks of production theory.

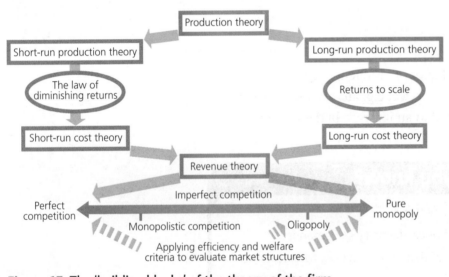

Figure 15 The 'building blocks' of the theory of the firm

Production and productivity

Production

- The total output of goods and services produced by an individual, firm or country.
- The process of converting inputs of raw materials and the factors of production, e.g. labour and capital machinery, into outputs.

Productivity

- Output per factor of production employed per unit of time.
- The formulae for measuring productivity are:

$$\text{productivity} = \frac{\text{total output per period of time}}{\text{number of units of factor of production}}$$

$$\text{labour productivity} = \frac{\text{total output per period of time}}{\text{number of units of labour}}$$

- Improvements in labour productivity can arise from better education and training and increased motivation.
- Advances in technology mean workers are equipped with the latest capital equipment, leading to increased labour productivity.
- Specialisation and division of labour facilitate more effective use of specialist capital equipment, leading to further increases in labour productivity.

Key terms

Production The total output of goods and services produced by an individual, firm or country.

Productivity A measurement of the rate of production by one or more factors of production.

Labour productivity Output per worker per unit of time.

Synoptic link

Productivity improvements are crucial to economic growth and international competitiveness.

Specialisation, division of labour and exchange

Specialisation

- Where an individual worker, firm, region or country produces a limited range of goods or services. For example:
  - an individual worker specialising as a tax accountant
  - an individual firm specialising in accountancy, e.g. PwC
  - an individual region specialising in investment banking, e.g. the City of London
  - an individual country specialising in the provision of financial services, e.g. the UK

Division of labour

- Specialisation at the level of the individual worker.

The importance of exchange

- Specialisation and division of labour are only viable if an efficient system of exchange exists, e.g. a tax accountant can exchange her services for payment so that she can buy food and pay her rent.
- A country such as the UK can only specialise in an output, e.g. financial services, if it is able to exchange this output for other goods and services which it is less able to produce efficiently, e.g. food.
- A system of exchange involving money as a medium of exchange avoids the need for barter and also has the benefit of easy divisibility.

Key terms

Specialisation Where an individual worker, firm, region or country produces a limited range of goods or services.

Division of labour Specialisation at the level of an individual worker.

Exchange Where one thing is traded for something else, e.g. an hour's work is given in return for a set payment.

Benefits of specialisation and division of labour

■ Repetition of a limited range of activities can increase skill and aptitude, leading to a worker becoming an expert, e.g. a leading neurosurgeon.
■ Reduced time spent moving between different tasks or workstations means increased productivity.
■ As tasks are broken up into smaller ones, it becomes efficient to use specialist machinery.
■ It allows people to work to their natural strengths.

Significance of the short run versus the long run

■ The **short run** is when at least one factor of production is fixed in quantity.
■ The **long run** is the period of time over which a firm can vary all of the factors of production and may increase or reduce its scale.

The law of diminishing returns and returns to scale

Diminishing returns

■ In the short run, costs may be influenced by **the law of diminishing returns**.
■ Figure 16 shows the law of diminishing returns as additional units of labour are added to a fixed factor, e.g. land or capital.

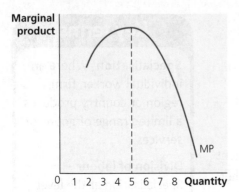

Figure 16 Marginal product increases and eventually decreases as diminishing returns set in

Costs of production in the long run
Returns to scale

Figure 17 contrasts short-run and long-run production.

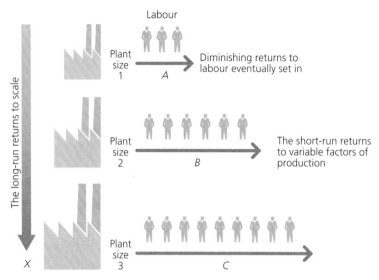

Figure 17 Contrasting short-run and long-run production

- In the long run, costs may be influenced by increasing or decreasing **returns to scale**.
- There are three possible scenarios:
  - ☐ **Increasing returns to scale**: an increase in the quantity of a firm's inputs leads to a proportionally greater change in output, e.g. a 5% increase in labour leads to a 10% increase in output.
  - ☐ **Constant returns to scale**: an increase in the quantity of a firm's inputs leads to a proportionally identical change in output, e.g. a 5% increase in labour leads to a 5% increase in output.
  - ☐ **Decreasing returns to scale**: an increase in the quantity of a firm's inputs leads to a proportionally lower change in output, e.g. a 10% increase in labour leads to a 5% increase in output.

> ## Key terms
>
> **Returns to scale** The relationship between increases in the quantity of a firm's inputs and the proportional change in output.
>
> **Fixed costs** Costs of production that do not vary with the level of output in the short run.

Costs of production
Fixed costs

- **Fixed costs** do not vary directly with output in the short run, e.g.:
  - ☐ rents on business premises
  - ☐ quarterly heating and lighting bills
  - ☐ salaries of senior staff
- Average fixed costs (AFC), however, fall as output increases, as the firm is able to spread the fixed costs over an increasing volume of output, as shown in Figure 18.

■ The formula for calculating average fixed costs is:

$$\text{average fixed costs (AFC)} = \frac{\text{total fixed costs}}{\text{output}}$$

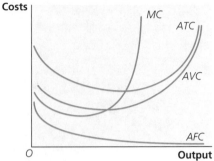

Figure 18 Short-run cost curves

Variable costs

■ **Variable costs** are those that vary directly with the level of output, e.g.:
  □ raw materials
  □ wages
  □ packaging
■ As shown in Figure 18, average variable costs (AVC) initially fall in the short run but begin to rise at higher levels of output.
■ The formula for calculating average variable costs is:

$$\text{average variable costs (AVC)} = \frac{\text{total variable costs}}{\text{output}}$$

Total costs

■ Total costs are made up of total fixed costs and total variable costs.
■ The formula is:

$$\text{total costs} = \text{total fixed costs} + \text{total variable costs}$$
$$\text{(TC)} \qquad \text{(TFC)} \qquad \text{(TVC)}$$

■ Average total costs, or costs per unit of output, are found by dividing total costs by total output. So:

$$\text{average total cost (ATC)} = \frac{\text{total costs (TC)}}{\text{output}}$$

■ Average total costs (ATC) = average fixed costs (AFC) + average variable costs (AVC), as shown in Figure 18.

Marginal cost

■ The addition to a firm's total costs from making an additional unit of output.

Key terms

Variable costs Costs of production that vary with the level of output.

Total cost The addition of fixed costs and variable costs at a given level of output.

Average cost Total costs of production divided by the number of units of output.

Marginal cost The addition to a firm's total costs from making an additional unit of output.

Exam tip

Make sure you know the difference between the short run and the long run and between fixed costs and variable costs.

- As increasing units of variable factors of production are added to a fixed factor in the short run, marginal cost of production initially declines and then begins to rise.
- The shape of the marginal cost curve, along with all short-run cost curves, is shown in Figure 18.

Economies and diseconomies of scale

Economies of scale

- The benefits of a firm increasing its output, leading to reduced average total costs.
- Figure 19 shows that, as a firm increases its output in the long run, average costs begin to fall up to output Q_1, due to the effect of one or more economies of scale.

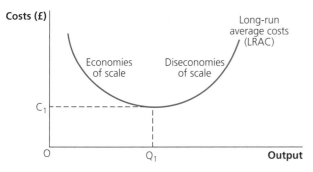

Figure 19 Long-run average cost curve

Internal and external economies of scale

- Internal economies of scale come about as a result of the growth of the firm itself, and include:
  1. financial economies of scale
  2. technical economies of scale
  3. marketing economies of scale
  4. managerial economies of scale
- External economies of scale occur when firms benefit from the growth of the industry in which they operate.

Diseconomies of scale

- When an increase in a firm's output leads to an increase in average costs of production — output levels beyond Q_1 in Figure 19.

Key terms

Economies of scale The reduced average total costs that firms experience by increasing output in the long run.

Internal economies of scale Reductions in long-run average total costs arising from growth of the firm.

External economies of scale Reductions in long-run average total costs arising from growth of the industry in which a firm operates.

Diseconomies of scale Increases in average total costs that firms may experience by increasing output in the long run.

Exam tip

Be aware of a few examples of very large businesses that have suffered from diseconomies of scale. Large supermarkets and banks have arguably been affected in recent years.

- Possible sources of diseconomies of scale include problems with:
  - □ coordination and control
  - □ communication

The minimum efficient scale of production

- In Figure 19, the **minimum efficient scale** occurs at output Q_1.
- In industries where the MES occurs at a large scale of output, only large firms will be able to achieve this, which can be a significant barrier to entry, leading to the dominance of one or a small number of powerful firms.

Marginal, average revenue and total revenue

- **Total revenue** (TR) is found by multiplying price (P) × quantity (Q) sold (or demanded).
- The formula is:

$$TR = P \times Q$$

- Figure 20 shows how total revenue changes as price changes.

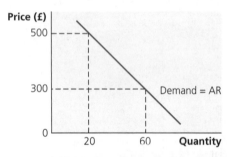

Price (£)

500

300

Demand = AR

0

20   60   **Quantity**

Figure 20 Total revenue, average revenue and the demand curve

- In order to calculate **average revenue** (AR), total revenue (TR) is divided by the quantity sold (Q).
- The formula is:

$$AR = \frac{TR}{Q}$$

- Average revenue is the same as price.
- Average revenue shows the quantity demanded at each price: the demand curve is also the average revenue curve.
- **Marginal revenue** (MR) is the addition to a firm's total revenue from selling an additional unit of output.

Market structure and marginal and average revenue

Perfect competition

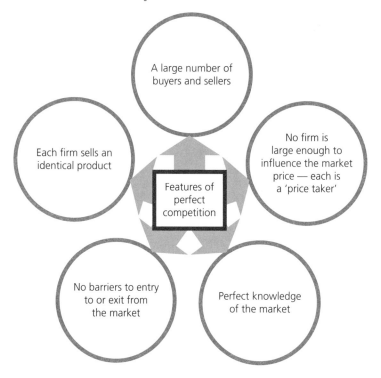

- Firms in perfect competition face a perfectly elastic demand curve.
- A constant price means that both average revenue (AR) and marginal revenue (MR) are constant.

Monopoly

- The pure monopolist's demand curve is effectively the entire market demand curve (not the case for a firm in perfect competition).
- The monopolist's demand curve is downward-sloping. In line with the law of demand, the monopolist has to reduce price to bring about an increase in quantity demanded.
- The monopolist's demand curve is also its AR curve.
- The monopolist's MR curve slopes downwards twice as steeply as the AR curve, as shown in Figure 21.
- Because the market demand or average revenue curve falls as output increases, the firm's marginal revenue curve must be below the average revenue curve.

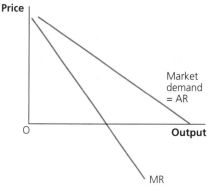

Figure 21 A monopolist faces downward-sloping demand, average and marginal revenue curves

Profit

- Total profit = total revenue − total costs.
- If this figure is negative, a loss is made.
- Profit creates an incentive for entrepreneurs to take a business risk.

Exam tip

Don't confuse profit with revenue. Profit takes costs away from total revenue.

Key terms

Profit The difference between total revenue and total costs.

Normal profit The minimum level of profit required to reward the entrepreneur for taking a risk and therefore to stay in a particular line of business.

Supernormal profit Profit over and above normal profit, sometimes referred to as abnormal or excess profit.

Technological change

- Arises out of inventions and innovations.
- Can affect methods of production, productivity and efficiency.
- Can lead to development of new products and markets and destruction of existing markets.
- **Invention** is the creation of a product or process; **innovation** is the improvement or development of an existing product, bringing it to market.
- Effects of technological change on a firm's long-run costs of production are shown in Figure 22. Long-run average total costs are reduced, reflecting dynamic efficiency.
- Technological change can make some markets more competitive, e.g. in the case of the internet, and others less competitive if the technology is protected by a patent.

Key terms

Invention The creation of a product or process.

Innovation New products and production processes that are developed into marketable good, or services.

Creative destruction Where technological change leads to the development of new, 'disruptive' products which render existing products obsolete.

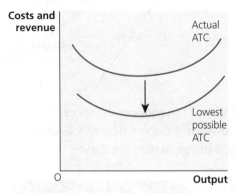

Figure 22 The effects of technological change on a firm's long-run costs of production

Creative destruction

■ Linked to technological change.
■ Monopoly power can easily be eroded by the development of new 'disruptive' technologies that effectively create new markets or revolutionise old ones.

Do you know?

1 Explain the difference between production and productivity.

2 With the aid of a diagram, explain the law of diminishing returns.

3 With the aid of a diagram, explain economies of scale, minimum efficient scale and diseconomies of scale.

4 State three internal economies of scale.

5 Draw a diagram showing marginal cost, average fixed cost, average variable cost and average total cost.

6 Explain the concept of creative destruction and how it may be linked to technological change.

1.5 Perfect competition, imperfectly competitive markets and monopoly

You need to know

■ market structures
■ the objectives of firms
■ perfect competition
■ monopolistic competition
■ oligopoly
■ monopoly and monopoly power
■ price discrimination, consumer and producer surplus
■ the competitive market process
■ contestable and non-contestable markets
■ market structure, static efficiency, dynamic efficiency and resource allocation

Market structure

- Some markets are supplied by a large number of small firms, e.g. commodities such as wheat.
- Other markets are supplied by one firm, or a small number of firms, e.g. internet search engines such as Google.

The spectrum of competition

- As shown in Figure 23, this ranges from perfect competition at one end to pure monopoly at the other end.
- **Perfect competition** is the most competitive form of market structure.
- **Pure monopoly** exists when only one firm supplies the market and is the least competitive form of market.

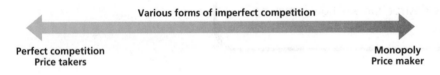

Various forms of imperfect competition

Perfect competition
Price takers

Monopoly
Price maker

Figure 23 A spectrum of competition

> ### Key terms
>
> **Market structure** The number and size of firms within a market for a particular good or service.
>
> **Perfect competition** A market structure that has a large number of buyers and sellers who have perfect information about the market, identical products and few, if any, barriers to entry.
>
> **Imperfect competition** Any market structure that is not perfect competition.
>
> **Pure monopoly** When only one firm supplies the market.

Objectives of firms

Profit maximisation

- The main objective of firms is maximising profit, i.e. making the maximum positive difference between costs and revenues.
- Making large profits enables firms to:
  - □ re-invest funds into developing new products that lead them to gain more customers
  - □ pay out higher returns to shareholders, which may encourage more people to buy shares in the company or help boost the share price
- Profit maximisation occurs when a firm's total revenue (TR) exceeds its total costs (TC) by the greatest amount.
- The profit-maximising rule for firms in all market structures is to produce the level of output where marginal cost (MC) = marginal revenue (MR).
- As shown in Figure 24, as MC meets MR from below, at output M_1, profit is maximised.
- While MC is also equal to MR at output M, crucially this is the profit minimisation or loss maximisation level of output, as the cost of every unit of output up to this point has exceeded the addition to total revenue.

> ### Exam tip
>
> Note that the profit-maximising rule for every firm in each type of market structure is MC = MR.

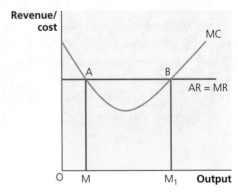

Figure 24 The profit-maximising rule for a firm in perfect competition

- Between output M and M_1, the addition to total revenue exceeds the addition to total cost.

Possible consequences of a divorce of ownership from control

- Separation of ownership from control may lead to conflicting objectives, with directors pursuing their own objectives and with profit maximisation, the assumed shareholder objective, not being a top priority.
- Objectives of directors, who run the business on a day-to-day basis, may include:
  - ☐ growth maximisation
  - ☐ sales revenue maximisation
  - ☐ **satisficing**
- In Figure 25, profit maximisation occurs at a single, specific output, Q_1, which will be hard to achieve.
- Satisfactory profits (P_{sat}) can be achieved at any level of output between Q_2 and Q_3.

Sales maximisation

- When firms' sales revenue is at a maximum.
- Occurs at the level of output where the sale of one more unit would not add to overall revenue.
- Can help a firm benefit from economies of scale.

Survival

- In its early stages of life, a firm might aim to survive the critical period before it establishes a customer base and repeat sales and is able to cover its costs.

Growth

- Once a firm has survived its first few critical years, its owners are likely to pursue an objective of growth.
- This will involve a firm increasing its output and scale of operation, meaning that it may be able to take advantage of various economies of scale.
- This will also help a business fend off takeover bids from rival companies.

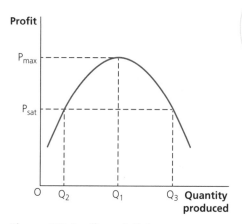

Figure 25 Profit satisficing

Key terms

Divorce of ownership from control The separation that exists between owners of the firm (shareholders) and directors in large public limited companies.

Satisficing Making do with a satisfactory, sub-optimal level of profit.

Exam tip

Don't confuse profit maximisation with sales revenue maximisation.

Increasing market share

- This is linked to the objective of growth.
- Having the highest market share for a particular product can give a firm the benefits of monopoly power, although this may also attract attention from the government, which may fear abuse of power.

Stakeholder objectives

- A modern view is that firms may achieve financial and non-financial objectives at the same time, e.g. looking after employee needs is at least as important as maximising profit.

Perfect competition

Price determination in highly competitive markets

Supply and demand analysis (Figure 26) shows how perfect competition works.

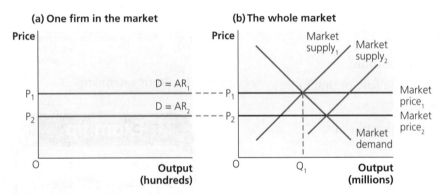

(a) One firm in the market **(b) The whole market**

Figure 26 Price determination in highly competitive markets

- Figure 26(a) shows a highly competitive market in which all firms are **price takers**. The firms supplying this market are initially earning supernormal profits. Market equilibrium price is P_1 and market output is Q_1.
- If other firms become aware that the existing firms in the market are earning supernormal profits, they will enter the market easily due to the low barriers to entry.
- This will have the effect of increasing overall supply in the market, as shown in Figure 26(b), which leads to a rightward shift of the market supply curve.
- This reduces the equilibrium price to P_2 as output increases beyond Q_1.
- This increase in supply and reduction in price will occur up to the point at which only normal profit is made, meaning that only the most competitive firms survive in the market.

■ In the short run it is possible for a firm to be making a loss, normal profit or supernormal profit. The latter case is shown in Figure 27.

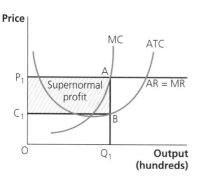

Figure 27 **Short-run profit maximisation under perfect competition**

Perfect competition in the long run

■ Perfectly competitive firms make normal profit in the long run only.
■ Any supernormal profit encourages firms to enter the industry, increasing market supply, while firms making losses will leave the market in the long run.
■ Only firms making normal profit remain in the market, illustrated in Figure 28, with individual firms producing at the profit-maximising output Q_1 and price P_1.
■ In the long term, firms in perfect competition are both productively efficient and allocatively efficient.

Advantages of perfect competition

■ **Static efficiency**, which consists of:
  □ **Productive efficiency** — firms that do not achieve this lose market share to rival firms who can produce the same product more cheaply.
  □ **Allocative efficiency** — highly competitive markets lead to firms producing what consumers demand since, if they do not, they will lose market share to firms which are producing the most desired products. This leads to consumer sovereignty.

Monopolistic competition

■ The features of monopolistic competition comprise:
  □ large number of producers
  □ similar products differentiated from one another, e.g. by branding or quality

Exam tips

■ While there are few, if any, real-world examples of perfect competition, the model provides a yardstick in both product and labour markets for judging the extent to which markets perform efficiently or inefficiently, and the extent to which a misallocation of resources occurs.
■ You should be able to critically assess the proposition that perfectly competitive markets lead to an efficient allocation of resources.

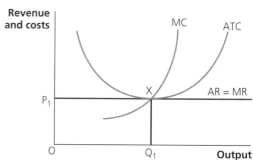

Figure 28 **Long-run profit maximisation under perfect competition**

Key terms

Static efficiency
Efficiency measured at a point in time, comprising productive efficiency and allocative efficiency.

Monopolistic competition
A form of imperfect competition with a large number of firms producing slightly differentiated products.

■ Examples include independent fast-food takeaways, plumbers and hairdressers.

In the short run

■ The short-run profit-maximising situation facing a firm in monopolistic competition is like that of the monopolist, with some brand loyalty leading to a downward-sloping demand curve, as shown in Figure 29.

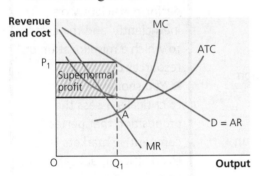

Figure 29 A firm in monopolistic competition in the short run

■ Firms maximise profit where MC = MR, at output Q_1, leading to an equilibrium price of P_1.
■ Firms can make supernormal profit equal to the shaded area.

In the long run

■ Firms make only normal profit.
■ Low barriers to entry mean new firms can enter an industry relatively easily, attracted by supernormal profits made by some firms.
■ This reduces demand (D = AR) for the individual firm, as new entrants take some market share.
■ Figure 30 illustrates a firm in monopolistic competition in the long run.
■ The D = AR curve is just tangential to the firm's ATC curve, meaning normal profit is made at the profit-maximising output Q_1.

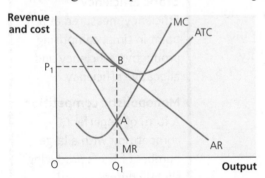

Figure 30 A firm in monopolistic competition in the long run

Exam tips

■ Don't confuse monopolistic competition with monopoly. The characteristics of monopolistic competition place it closer to perfect competition than monopoly in terms of market structure.
■ Remember that the profit-maximising level of output for all forms of market structure occurs where MC = MR.

Oligopoly

- Where a small number of relatively powerful firms compete for market share.
- Markets tend to be highly concentrated.
- Firms are interdependent.

Concentration ratios

- The total market share held by the largest firms in the industry.

Collusive and non-collusive oligopoly

- Collusion occurs when firms work together to determine price and/or output.
- This reduces uncertainty that may exist among firms in the industry regarding pricing and output decisions of rivals.
- A **cartel** is a collusive arrangement where oligopoly firms agree to fix prices and/or output between themselves.
- Collusion between firms can be either **tacit** or **overt**.
- Where collusive agreements are made, consumers are presented with an effective monopoly.

The kinked demand curve model of oligopoly

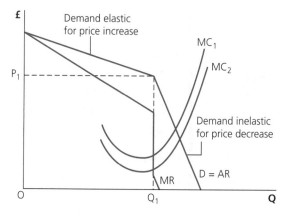

Figure 31 The kinked demand curve model of oligopoly

- The model illustrates the **interdependence** and uncertainty facing firms and why oligopolistic markets tend to have stable prices and non-price methods of competition.
- If an individual firm produces at Q_1 in Figure 31, selling at price P_1, it perceives its demand curve as being relatively elastic if it raises its price and inelastic if it cuts its price.
- Firms expect not to follow a price rise but to follow a price cut.

Exam tip

Oligopolistic markets can vary in relation to the number of firms, degree of product differentiation and ease of entry.

- If a firm increases its price and rivals do not follow suit, it loses some, but not all, market share.
- If a firm cuts its price, other firms have no option but to follow — leading to a small expansion of market size but no increase in market share for the individual firm.
- Firms in oligopoly therefore prefer non-price forms of competition.

Methods of non-price competition

- Product differentiation, e.g. packaging and advertising
- Customer service, e.g. after-sales service
- Loyalty products, e.g. loyalty cards

Monopoly and monopoly power

- Pure monopoly exists when there is a single supplier of a good or service, i.e. 100% market share. The firm is a **price maker**.
- A firm needn't have a pure monopoly to exert monopoly power; there are many industries dominated by a small number of firms with monopoly power.
- Barriers to entry tend to be high.
- Firms restrict output to raise price, which boosts supernormal profits.
- Barriers to entry mean that firms can maintain these profits because new firms can't easily enter the market to compete profits away.

Profit maximisation under monopoly

- The profit-maximising equilibrium situation for a monopolist is shown in Figure 32.
- As in all market structures, the monopolist maximises profit at the level of output at which MC = MR, i.e. at Q_1.
- Firms make supernormal profit equal to the shaded area.

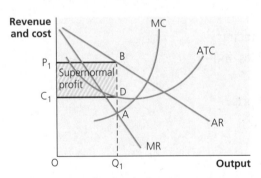

Figure 32 Profit maximisation under monopoly

Barriers to entry

■ Features of a market that make it difficult for new firms to enter that market and can therefore lead to **monopoly power**.

Type of barrier	Description	Example
Natural barriers	Include naturally-occurring climatic, geographical or geological factors that make the product difficult to replicate elsewhere	Wine-growing regions
Economies of scale	When a firm's average costs of production fall as output increases	Large firms can set their prices below those of any potential new entrant firms to the market, and still make a supernormal profit
Legal barriers	Factors which give a single firm or individual the right to have a monopoly over a new product, process or other intellectual property, either forever or over a given time	Patents, copyrights and trademarks
Product differentiation	Existing firms in a market may have spent considerable sums of money over many years on advertising and branding in order to build up a significant consumer loyalty and marketing profile	The large advertising budgets of major soft drinks firms
Sunk costs	Costs that cannot easily be recovered if a firm is unsuccessful in a market and has to exit, i.e. these financial commitments are essentially lost, or 'sunk'	Market research costs

Concentrated markets

■ Monopolies and oligopolies (close to monopoly on the spectrum of competition), i.e. markets dominated by a small number of firms.

Advantages and disadvantages of monopoly

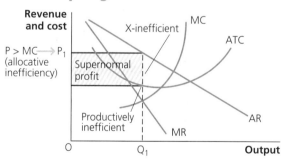

Figure 33 Productive, allocative and x-inefficiency under monopoly

Advantages	Disadvantages
■ Economies of scale: □ financial □ technical □ marketing □ managerial ■ Innovation	■ Productive and allocative inefficiency ■ X-inefficiency ■ Diseconomies of scale

Key terms

Concentrated market A market dominated by a small number of firms.

X-inefficiency The lack of willingness of firms with monopoly power to control their costs of production.

Innovation New products and production processes that are developed into marketable goods or services.

Natural monopoly A market where a single firm can benefit from continuous economies of scale.

Natural monopoly

- Where it is uneconomic for more than one firm to supply a market because that firm enjoys continuous economies of scale, e.g. utilities such as household gas.
- It is productively efficient for a single firm to supply the market, as several individual firms can't achieve the low costs of the single firm.
- If the market were broken up, average costs would be higher than for a single firm, meaning prices may be higher.

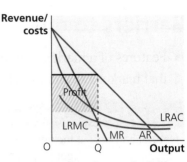

Figure 34 Continuously falling long-run average costs under natural monopoly

Price discrimination, consumer and producer surplus

Conditions necessary for price discrimination

- Firms must have a degree of monopoly power.
- Different sub-markets of consumers with different elasticities of demand.
- No 'seepage' between markets — consumers being charged higher prices mustn't be able to access cheaper prices.

Consumer and producer surplus

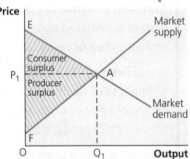

Figure 35 Illustrating consumer surplus and producer surplus

- Concepts of economic welfare.
- **Consumer surplus** is the surplus value or satisfaction consumers enjoy. In Figure 35, this is equal to the area given by the triangle P_1EA.
- **Producer surplus** may be regarded as surplus value enjoyed by producers. This is equal to the area given by the triangle P_1AF in Figure 35.
- Figure 36 shows the effects of price discrimination on the profits of a firm with monopoly power.

> ### Exam tip
> The concepts of consumer and producer surplus are important in an analysis of the impact on economic welfare of price and output changes.

> ### Key terms
> **Price discrimination** Where firms with monopoly power charge different groups of consumers different prices for the same product.
>
> **Consumer surplus** The difference between what a consumer would be prepared to pay and the price they actually pay for a good or service.
>
> **Producer surplus** The difference between what a firm would be willing to accept for a good or service and what they actually receive.

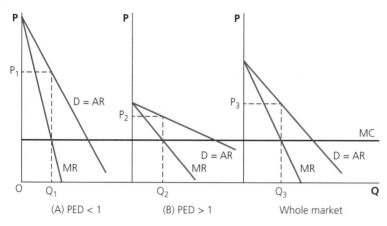

Figure 36 The effects of price discrimination on the profits of a firm with monopoly power

Advantages of price discrimination	Disadvantages of price discrimination
<ul><li>Supernormal profits may be re-invested by the price-discriminating firm, leading to better quality products</li><li>Extra profits can 'subsidise' those paying a lower price</li><li>Those on lower incomes can access services, e.g. lower-priced off-peak train fares</li></ul>	<ul><li>Earning or increasing supernormal profit can be seen as inequitable</li><li>Increases producer surplus at the expense of consumer surplus</li><li>May be seen as exploiting those in greatest need who have no choice about using peak-time services</li></ul>

> **Exam tip**
>
> Price discrimination isn't always bad for consumers and producers. It may be used to cross-subsidise cheaper prices for less well-off members of society, for example.

The competitive market process

How firms in concentrated markets behave

Price competition

- Firms may benefit from economies of scale, which reduce average costs of production, so they could reduce prices while still making supernormal profit.
- Firms may make use of these profits to re-invest into researching and developing new, innovative products and production methods.
- Dynamic efficiency leads to a reduction in the firms' costs at every given output level.
- If a firm wishes to take market share from rivals, it may initiate a **price war** by undercutting others.

Non-price competition

- Firms in highly concentrated markets compete vigorously with one another on the basis of factors other than price, e.g. quality of service.

> **Key terms**
>
> **Price competition** Reducing the price of a good or service in order to make it more attractive than those of competitors.
>
> **Price war** Where firms in an industry repeatedly cut prices below those of competitors in order to win market share.
>
> **Non-price competition** Competition on the basis of product features other than price, such as quality, advertising or after-sales service.

Dynamics of competition and competitive market processes

- Firms in concentrated markets may compete on both price and/or non-price factors.
- Large firms may use economies of scale to reduce their prices, taking market share from rival firms.
- Firms often compete using non-price factors such as quality, reliability and strategies to increase consumer loyalty.
- Over time, creative destruction happens: firms in monopoly use innovation to overcome existing barriers to entry, often in dramatic ways.

Contestable and non-contestable markets

- **Contestable markets** are those where barriers to entry and exit can be overcome.
- Making markets more contestable could lead to incumbent firms behaving in more economically desirable ways with regard to pricing and static efficiency.

Features of perfectly contestable markets

- freedom of entry to and exit from the market
- no sunk costs
- perfect information
- firms produce where price = marginal cost

Impact of contestable markets

- May lead to incumbent firms behaving in more economically desirable ways with regard to pricing and static efficiency, otherwise new entrants would be taking a share of any supernormal profits (**hit and run competition**).
- Figure 37 shows the effects of contestability on the price, output and profit of a firm with monopoly power.
- The firm would price at P_C and produce at output Q_C, making only normal profit. This is in contrast to the usual profit-maximising price and output of a monopolist at P_M and Q_M.

Key terms

Contestable market A market with freedom of entry and exit.

Hit and run competition In contestable markets, where new entrants take a share of the supernormal profits and then exit the industry.

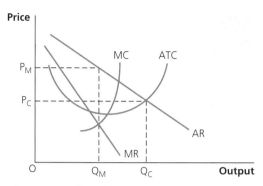

Figure 37 The effects of contestability on price, output and profit

Static efficiency and dynamic efficiency

- The performance of different market structures can be judged by the extent to which they are statically efficient or dynamically efficient.
- Perfect competition performs well in terms of static efficiency but not **dynamic efficiency**.
- Static efficiency in perfect competition is shown in Figure 38.

> **Key term**
>
> **Dynamic efficiency** Improvements in productive efficiency over time.

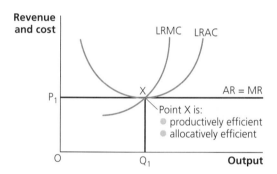

Figure 38 Static efficiency in perfect competition

- Dynamic efficiency arises from improvements in productive efficiency over time, e.g. technology.
- Larger firms in either oligopoly or monopoly may have easier access to the financial resources necessary to be dynamically efficient, i.e. from supernormal profits.
- They may also have strong incentives to become so if there are competitive pressures in their industry.
- Dynamic efficiency is shown in Figure 39, with a reduction in long-run average costs from LRAC$_1$ to LRAC$_2$, leading to a fall in cost at every level of output.

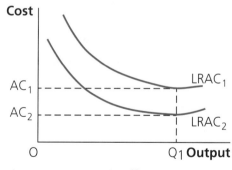

Figure 39 Dynamic efficiency

Do you know?

1 State three features of each of these market structures: perfect competition, monopolistic competition, oligopoly, monopoly.

2 Explain what is meant by a divorce of ownership from control.

3 State and explain three possible objectives of firms.

4 Using a diagram, explain how a firm in perfect competition can be productively and allocatively efficient in the long run.

5 Using at least one diagram, explain the difference between the short run and long run for a firm in monopolistic competition.

6 Using a diagram, explain how oligopolistic firms may be affected by interdependence.

7 Using a diagram, explain how price discrimination can increase the profits of a monopolist.

1.6 The labour market

You need to know
- the demand for labour
- influences on the supply of labour to different markets
- wage differentials
- the determination of relative wage rates and levels of employment in perfectly competitive labour markets
- the determination of relative wage rates and levels of employment in imperfectly competitive labour markets
- the influence of trade unions in determining wages and levels of employment
- the national minimum wage
- discrimination in the labour market

Figure 40 shows the link between the goods market, covered in earlier sections, and the labour market.

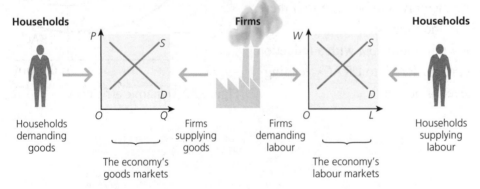

Figure 40 The goods market and the labour market, which is one of the economy's factor markets

The demand for labour

Derived demand

- The demand for factors of production, such as labour, is derived from the demand for the product they are used to create.

Marginal productivity theory

- The demand for labour is also known as the theory of **marginal revenue productivity (MRP)**.
- A firm's demand for labour depends on the productivity of additional units of labour, known as **marginal physical product (MPP)**, multiplied by the selling price of the product.
- MRP is the addition to a firm's revenue from employing an additional unit of labour.
- The demand curve for labour, usually referred to as the MRP curve, shows the relationship between the wage rate and the number of workers employed.
- In a perfectly competitive product market, MR is constant and therefore the gradients of the MPP and MRP curves will be the same.

Determinants of labour demand

- wage rates
- labour productivity
- the price of substitute factors
- other labour costs

A change in wage rate will lead to a movement along the demand curve for labour, while a change in the other determinants will lead to a shift of the demand curve for labour.

Determinants of elasticity of demand for labour

The formula is:

elasticity of demand for labour =

$$\frac{\text{percentage change in quantity of labour demanded}}{\text{percentage change in wage rate}}$$

Factors determining the elasticity of demand for labour:

- ease of substitution
- time
- elasticity of demand for the good or service
- proportion of labour cost to total cost of production

> ### Key terms
>
> **Marginal revenue productivity (MRP)** The addition to a firm's revenue from employing an additional unit of a factor of production, usually labour.
>
> **Marginal physical product (MPP)** The addition to output from employing an additional unit of a factor of production, usually labour.

> ### Exam tip
>
> Don't confuse a movement along a demand curve for labour, caused by a change in wage rate, with a shift of the demand curve for labour, caused by other factors.

> ### Key term
>
> **Elasticity of demand for labour** A measure of the responsiveness of the quantity of labour demanded following a change in the wage rate.

Influences on the supply of labour to different markets

Supply of labour to a particular occupation

- The supply curve for labour shows the relationship between the wage rate and number of workers willing and able to work in a particular occupation.
- It is influenced by monetary factors such as the wage rate, and non-monetary factors such as job satisfaction and working conditions.
- Monetary and non-monetary factors taken together are known as net advantage.
- A worker who is free to decide how many hours to work each day or week can maximise their net advantage by choosing between supplying more labour or enjoying more leisure time.

Determinants of supply of labour

- wage rates
- size of working population
- non-monetary factors

A change in wage rate will lead to a movement along the supply curve for labour.

A change in the other determinants will lead to a shift of the supply curve for labour.

Determinants of elasticity of supply of labour

The formula is:

elasticity of supply of labour =

$$\frac{\text{percentage change in quantity of labour supplied}}{\text{percentage change in wage rate}}$$

Factors determining the elasticity of supply of labour:

- time
- length of training period
- vocation

The difference between elastic and inelastic supply for labour is highlighted in Figure 41.

Exam tip

Workers will take into account the monetary and non-monetary features of a job when deciding to supply their labour, a concept referred to as 'net advantage'. Good non-monetary factors may compensate for relatively poor pay, and vice versa.

Key term

Elasticity of supply of labour A measure of the responsiveness of the quantity of labour supplied following a change in the wage rate.

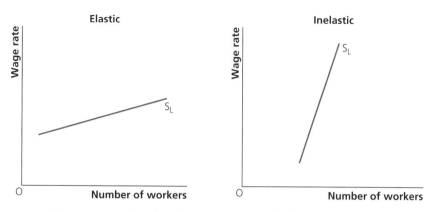

Figure 41 Elastic and inelastic supply curves for labour

Wage differentials

- The factors determining the extent and elasticities of demand and supply for labour can be put together to explain why some groups of workers earn more or less than others.

Perfectly competitive labour markets

- each unit of labour is identical in skill and unable to influence the wage rate
- workers must accept the going wage rate, determined by supply and demand at market level
- individual firms are wage takers
- individual firms maximise profit by employing the quantity of labour at which $MRP = MC$ (the wage rate)
- perfect information
- freedom of entry to and exit from the industry

In a perfectly competitive labour market, each individual employer has to accept the ruling market wage, as shown in the right-hand diagram in Figure 42.

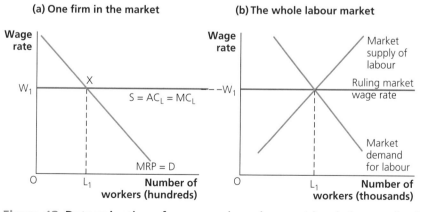

Figure 42 Determination of wages and employment levels in a perfectly competitive labour market

Key term

Wage differentials
Differences in wages arising between individuals, occupations, industries and regions.

Synoptic link

Wage differentials are a reason for differences in income and wealth, and relative poverty.

Exam tip

It is helpful to be able to use economic theory to explain wage differentials.

Imperfectly competitive labour markets

Monopsony

- A labour market with a single dominant buyer of workers, e.g. government and teachers.
- Employers use market power to reduce the wage rate and level of employment below those of a perfectly competitive labour market.
- The marginal cost (MC) of employing workers exceeds the average cost (AC).
- To attract an additional worker, the firm has to pay more to this worker as well as to all other employees.
- Figure 43 shows equilibrium in a monopsony labour market.
- In order to maximise profit, the monopsonist employs workers where MRP = MC, which results in a wage rate of W_1 and Q_1 of labour employed.
- Wage rate and level of employment are both below those in a competitive labour market.

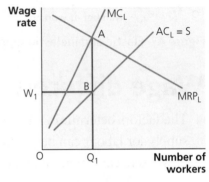

Figure 43 The equilibrium position in a monopsony labour market

Influence of trade unions

- **Trade unions** are organisations of workers set up to further the interests of members through bargaining collectively with employers.
- This gives workers power to set wages higher than otherwise.

Trade unions introduced to previously competitive labour markets

- Will increase wages for those who keep their jobs, but reduce employment levels.
- Figure 44 illustrates the effects of introducing a trade union to a competitive labour market.
- The competitive wage rate before the introduction of a trade union is W_1, with Q_1 workers employed.
- If employees join a trade union they are able to negotiate a higher wage of W_2, with Q_3 workers willing to supply their labour at this wage.

Key terms

Monopsony A market with a single dominant buyer, such as the government in relation to state school teachers.

Trade union A group of workers that bargains collectively with employers to increase its members' wages.

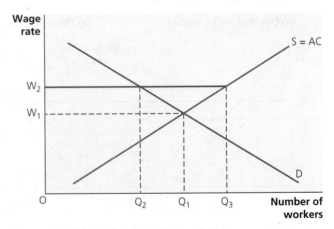

Figure 44 The effects of introducing a trade union into a previously competitive labour market

- However, the firm is willing to demand only Q_2 of labour at this higher wage, leading to excess supply of workers of $Q_3 - Q_2$, which is effectively unemployment.
- The introduction of a trade union to a previously competitive labour market results in additional unemployment of $Q_1 - Q_2$.

Trade unions in imperfectly competitive labour markets

- The introduction of a trade union to a monopsony increases wage rate and level of employment.
- Figure 45 illustrates the effects of introducing a trade union to a monopsony labour market, an example of a bilateral monopoly.
- The trade union manages to increase the wage rate (W_2) and the level of employment (Q_2) compared to the monopsony situation without a trade union (W_1 and Q_1).

The national minimum wage

- The **national minimum wage** (NMW) legally obliges employers to pay workers at least a certain hourly rate.
- Depending on the elasticities of demand and supply for labour, the introduction or raising of the NMW may have significant impacts on employment levels.
- The effects of introducing a NMW are illustrated in Figure 46.
- The free market equilibrium wage and quantity of labour employed are W_1 and Q_1 respectively. A minimum wage introduced above the free market wage, e.g. at W_2, would lead to an excess supply of labour equal to $Q_3 - Q_2$, which would be unemployment.

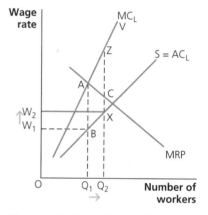

Figure 45 The effects of introducing a trade union to a monopsony labour market

Key term

National minimum wage (NMW) a statutory minimum wage used to increase the earnings of the low-paid.

Exam tip

Figure 46 is similar to the analysis of the effects of the introduction of a national minimum wage above the market equilibrium wage.

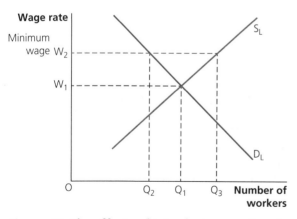

Figure 46 The effects of introducing a national minimum wage

Discrimination in the labour market

- Where employers under-value or over-value the marginal revenue productivity (MRP) of certain groups of workers for reasons such as ethnicity, gender or age.
- Under-valuation of MRP is known as **negative discrimination**, while over-valuation is known as **positive discrimination**.
- Leads to market failure and impacts on wages and levels of employment.

Conditions necessary for wage discrimination

- firms must have some wage-setting ability, i.e. an imperfect labour market
- distinct/separate labour markets
- lack of legal protection or imperfect information on the part of the government

Figure 47 shows the effects of wage discrimination on labour markets.

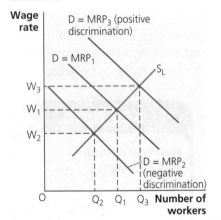

Figure 47 **The effects of wage discrimination on labour markets**

Economic disadvantages of wage discrimination	Economic advantages of wage discrimination
- May lead to some groups being underpaid and under-employed, worsening relative poverty - Increased government spending on welfare benefits - Waste of scarce, valuable resources - May lead to increased litigation as workers attempt to take legal action against employers - Lack of cultural diversity in the workplace - May create social tensions	- Firms can reduce their wage bills and therefore be more competitive - May be beneficial to some firms if their consumers are racially prejudiced

Do you know?

1 Explain how marginal revenue productivity determines the demand for labour.

2 State three reasons why the demand curve for labour might shift to the right.

3 State three reasons why the supply curve for labour might shift to the left.

4 Explain how wages and employment are determined in a perfectly competitive labour market.

5 Using a diagram, explain how a trade union may affect wages and employment in a monopsony labour market.

6 Using a diagram, explain the impact of increasing the national minimum wage.

1.7 The distribution of income and wealth: poverty and inequality

You need to know

- the distribution of income and wealth
- the problem of poverty
- government policies to alleviate poverty and to influence the distribution of income and wealth

Distribution of income and wealth

The difference between income and wealth

Key terms

Income A flow of money to a factor of production, usually labour.

Wealth A stock of valuable assets such as property or shares.

■ Both are unequally distributed between households in the UK.

Factors leading to an unequal distribution of income

- differences in skills, qualifications and work experience
- differences in wealth
- impact of the state

Factors leading to an unequal distribution of wealth

- differences in income
- inheritance
- marriage
- property

Equality versus equity

- Equality means that income and wealth are shared out equally between all members of society, whereas equity is the notion of fairness.

Measuring inequality

The Lorenz curve

- This is a diagram measuring and illustrating income or wealth inequality.
- The further the Lorenz curve is from the 45° line of perfect equality, the greater the inequality, as shown in Figure 48.

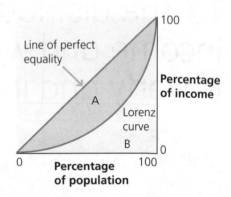

Figure 48 A Lorenz curve

The Gini coefficient

- The Gini coefficient is a statistical measure of the degree of inequality.
- It is the ratio of the area between the 45° line and the Lorenz curve divided by the total area below the 45° line. Referring to Figure 49, this is calculated by the formula:

$$\text{Gini coefficient} = \frac{\text{area A}}{\text{area A} + \text{B}}$$

  - □ The higher the value, the more inequality exists.
  - □ Perfect equality gives a Gini coefficient of 0.
  - □ Perfect inequality gives a Gini coefficient of 1.

Possible costs of income and wealth inequality

- Social tensions
- The creation of an 'underclass'

Possible benefits of income and wealth inequality

- Incentive effects
- Trickle-down

> ### Key term
>
> **Trickle-down** A free market view that poorer members of society will benefit from high earners and the relatively wealthy, e.g. through job opportunities and helping to fund merit goods.

The problem of poverty

- Inequality in the distribution of income and wealth can lead to poverty, which can be either relative or absolute.

The difference between relative and absolute poverty

> ### Key terms
>
> **Relative poverty** When some people in society are worse off than others, e.g. earning less than 60% of a country's median income.
>
> **Absolute poverty** When some people can't afford the basic necessities to sustain life, e.g. food, shelter and warmth.

Causes and effects of poverty

Causes of poverty	Effects of poverty
<ul><li>relatively low wages</li><li>unemployment</li><li>regressive taxation</li><li>old age</li><li>imperfect information</li></ul>	<ul><li>greater demands on the welfare system</li><li>poor educational attainment</li><li>poor health</li></ul>

Policies to alleviate poverty

- **Progressive taxes**: critics argue they create disincentives to work, leading to voluntary unemployment, slower economic growth and reduced income tax revenues.
- **National minimum wage**: critics argue that if the NMW is set too high, it could lead to increased unemployment.
- **Welfare benefits**: increasing benefits may increase the replacement ratio and reduce incentives to work.
- **Education and training**: an individual may take a long time to feel the positive impacts of education and training in terms of increased employability.
- **Reducing unemployment**: expansionary fiscal and monetary policies have time lags before their full effects are felt and may

also lead to demand-pull inflation, depending on the extent of supply-side inflexibilities.

■ **Promoting trickle-down**: critics of trickle-down argue that it doesn't really work, e.g. because the highest earners in society can afford the best tax accountants to help them minimise the tax they pay.

Do you know?

1 Explain the difference between income and wealth.

2 State three factors that may lead to an unequal distribution of income.

3 State three factors that may lead to an unequal distribution of wealth.

4 State two possible costs and two benefits of income and wealth inequality.

5 Explain the difference between relative and absolute poverty.

6 State and briefly explain three policies to alleviate poverty.

1.8 The market mechanism, market failure and government intervention in markets

You need to know

■ how markets and prices allocate resources
■ the meaning of market failure
■ the meaning of public goods, private goods and quasi-public goods
■ the meaning of externalities
■ the meaning of environmental market failure and the tragedy of the commons
■ the meaning of merit and demerit goods
■ the meaning of market imperfections
■ an inequitable distribution of income and wealth
■ government intervention in markets
■ competition policy

How markets and prices allocate resources

The four functions of prices

> ### Key terms
>
> **Rationing** Increasing prices rations demand to those most able to afford a good or service.
>
> **Signalling** Prices provide important information to market participants.
>
> **Incentive** Prices create incentives for market participants to change their actions.
>
> **Allocative** The function of prices that acts to divert resources to where returns can be maximised.

- When any of these key functions of prices breaks down, market failure is said to occur.

The meaning of market failure

- This is when a market fails to achieve productive efficiency, allocative efficiency or equity.

> ### Key terms
>
> **Market failure** When the free market leads to a misallocation of resources in an economy.
>
> **Complete market failure** When the free market fails to create a market for a good or service, also referred to as a missing market.
>
> **Partial market failure** When a market for a good or service exists, but it is consumed or produced in quantities that do not maximise economic welfare.

> ### Exam tip
>
> Make sure you understand the difference between complete and partial market failure.

Public goods, private goods and quasi-public goods

Public goods have two key characteristics:

- **Non-excludable**: non-paying customers cannot be excluded from consuming a good, once it has been produced.
- **Non-rival**: one person's enjoyment of the good does not diminish another person's enjoyment of the good.

> ### Key term
>
> **Public good** A good that is non-excludable and non-rival in consumption.

> ### Exam tip
>
> Make sure you understand the two key characteristics of public goods.

The free rider problem

■ Public goods are an example of complete market failure, as the free market would have no incentive to provide them.
■ This is the free rider problem: individual consumers hope to get a 'free ride' without paying for the benefit they enjoy.

Private goods

■ These are the opposite of public goods, i.e. they are excludable and rival.
■ Non-payers can be excluded from consuming a good, and consumption by one person diminishes the enjoyment of the good by another.

Quasi-public goods

■ Those which possess some, but not all, characteristics of a public good, i.e. they may be partially excludable, or partially rival.

Externalities

■ These are the knock-on effects of economic transactions on third parties.

■ The key points of understanding are:
  □ marginal **private cost** (MPC) + marginal external cost (MEC) = marginal **social cost** (MSC)
  □ marginal **private benefit** (MPB) + marginal external benefit (MEB) = marginal **social benefit** (MSB)
  □ social welfare is optimised when MSB = MSC

Positive externalities in production

■ The actions of firms have wider benefits to society, e.g. building a new airport runway.
■ In a free market, individual firms only take into account private costs and benefits and not those of wider society.
■ As shown in Figure 49, MPC > MSC, meaning there is a negative marginal external cost, equal to the vertical distance between the MPC and MSC curves at the free market equilibrium quantity, Q_1.
■ The social optimum quantity occurs where MSB = MSC, i.e. at Q_2; there is under-production of airport capacity equal to $Q_2 - Q_1$, leading to an overall welfare loss equal to the shaded triangle.

Key terms

Private good A good which is rival and excludable in consumption.

Quasi-public good A good which exhibits some, but not all, of the characteristics of a public good, i.e. it is partially non-excludable and/or partially non-rival.

Externality A knock-on effect of an economic transaction on third parties.

Private cost The cost to an individual producer involved in a market transaction.

Social cost The total of private cost plus external cost of an economic transaction.

Private benefit The benefit to an individual consumer involved in a market transaction.

Social benefit The total of private benefit plus external benefit of an economic transaction.

Positive externality A positive knock-on effect of an economic transaction on third parties, also known as an external benefit.

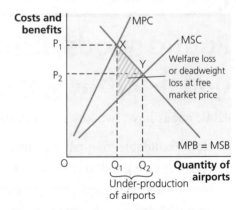

Figure 49 **Positive externalities in production**

Positive externalities in consumption

- The actions of individual consumers have wider benefits to society, e.g. taking regular exercise and eating healthy food.
- In a free market, individual consumers only take into account their private costs and benefits and not those of wider society.
- As shown in Figure 50, MSB > MPB, meaning there is a marginal external benefit, equal to the vertical distance between the MSB and MPB curves at the free market equilibrium quantity, Q_1.
- The social optimum quantity occurs where MSB = MSC, i.e. at Q_2; there is under-consumption of healthy food and exercise equal to $Q_2 - Q_1$, leading to an overall welfare loss equal to the shaded triangle.

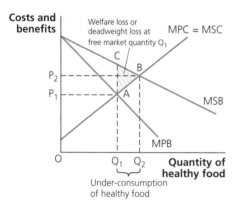

Figure 50 Positive externalities in consumption

Negative externalities in production

- The actions of firms have wider costs to society, e.g. a coastal oil refinery.
- In a free market, the individual firm only takes into account its private costs and benefits and not those of wider society.
- As shown in Figure 51, MSC > MPC, meaning there is a marginal external cost, equal to the vertical distance between the MSC and MPC curves at the free market equilibrium quantity, Q_1.
- The social optimum quantity occurs where MSB = MSC, i.e. at Q_2; there is over-production by the oil refinery equal to $Q_1 - Q_2$, leading to an overall welfare loss equal to the shaded triangle.

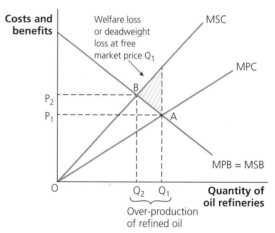

Figure 51 Negative externalities in production

Negative externalities in consumption

- The perceived benefits of consumption activities to individual consumers exceed the benefits to society, e.g. demerit goods such as alcohol.

- In a free market, the individual consumer only takes into account their private costs and benefits and not those of wider society.
- As shown in Figure 52, MPB > MSB, meaning there is a negative marginal external benefit, equal to the vertical distance between the MPB and MSB curves at the free market equilibrium quantity, Q_1.
- The social optimum quantity occurs where MSB = MSC, i.e. at Q_2; there is over-consumption of demerit goods equal to $Q_2 - Q_1$, leading to an overall welfare loss equal to the shaded triangle.

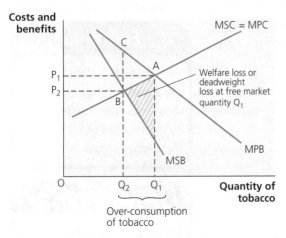

Figure 52 Negative externalities in consumption

Environmental market failure and the tragedy of the commons

Environmental market failure

- Negative externalities that lead to some form of environmental damage, e.g. over-use of non-renewable resources such as oil, coal and gas, or exploitation of the oceans, forests or atmosphere.
- One reason is a lack of clearly defined **property rights** relating to environmental resources.
- Economic agents do not suffer any penalty for polluting the atmosphere, e.g. dumping waste in the oceans, or excessive deforestation.
- This leads to over-use of these resources and the rapid depletion of non-renewable resources.

The tragedy of the commons

- Environmental market failures.
- Refers to the over-use of any natural resource, such as the oceans, forests, atmosphere or minerals in the ground.

Merit and demerit goods

Examples of **merit goods** include:

- education
- healthcare
- exercise
- car insurance
- healthy foods

There is some overlap between the concepts of a merit good and a positive externality in consumption.

Merit goods would be under-consumed in a free market, for several possible reasons:

- people aren't aware of the potential private benefits to themselves from consuming the merit good, especially in the long term
- they may not be able to afford the product
- they may not take into account the wider benefits to society of their use of merit goods

Examples of **demerit goods** include 'recreational' drugs, such as alcohol and tobacco, and other aspects of an unhealthy lifestyle, such as fatty, sugary foods.

Demerit goods would be over-consumed in a free market, and often give rise to negative externalities in consumption. Demerit goods are over-consumed because:

- people may not be aware of the damage to their health arising from consumption
- goods are too cheap and so people can too easily afford them, or they are too accessible
- individuals do not take account of the wider external costs associated with their consumption

> ### Key terms
>
> **Merit good** A good which would be under-consumed in a free market.
>
> **Demerit good** A good which would be over-consumed in a free market.

Market imperfections

Economists often make use of theoretical 'perfect' markets in order to make comparisons with markets in reality. Perfect markets have:

- perfect information
- no barriers to entry and exit
- homogeneous products and factors of production
- large numbers of buyers and sellers
- perfect mobility of factors of production

These features are clearly unrealistic and real-life markets tend to have a range of imperfections as outlined below.

Imperfect and asymmetric information

- **Imperfect information** exists when economic agents do not know everything they would need to know in order to make a fully informed decision.
- Individual consumers may not be fully aware of the positive and negative consequences of their use of certain goods, especially in the long term.
- As a result they may consume insufficient or excessive amounts in terms of maximising the overall welfare of society.
- **Asymmetric information** is a similar concept but implies that one economic agent knows more than another, giving that agent more power in the decision-making process.

Monopoly

Immobility of factors of production

- **Occupational immobility**: factors of production, especially labour, are unlikely to be perfectly mobile between different uses or occupations.
- **Geographical immobility**: individuals may not be aware of, or easily able to move to, where jobs exist.

An inequitable distribution of income and wealth

- **Equity** is the notion of fairness in the allocation of economic resources.
- In a market economy, with no government intervention, those with the highest incomes will tend to have access to the greatest share of resources.
- Free market capitalists argue that inequality creates incentives that positively influence overall national income and can 'trickle down' to poorer members of society, raising overall living standards.
- Critics of free market capitalism say inequality creates social tensions between the relatively rich and poor, leading to reduced living standards.

Key terms

Information failure A source of market failure where market participants do not have enough information to be able to make effective judgements about the 'correct' levels of consumption or production of a good.

Occupational immobility A source of factor immobility that means workers find it difficult to move between occupations for reasons of a lack of desirable skills.

Geographical immobility A source of factor immobility that means workers have difficulty in moving to locations where jobs are available for reasons such as a lack of affordable housing or family reasons.

Inequitable distribution of income and wealth When the way in which income and wealth are distributed in society is considered unfair.

Equity The notion of fairness in society.

Synoptic link

See Section 1.5 for an overview of monopoly.

Government intervention in markets

Reasons for government intervention

- To correct market failure.
- To achieve a fairer (or more equitable) distribution of income and wealth.
- To achieve the government's macroeconomic objectives.

Indirect taxation

- Increases the costs of firms: the supply curve shifts leftwards.
- The government can use two different types of indirect taxation:
  - □ specific or unit taxes — a fixed amount is added per unit of a good or service, e.g. bottles of alcohol
  - □ ad valorem taxes — involve adding a percentage of the price of a good or service, e.g. VAT at 20% would add 20p to a product costing £1, but £20 to a product costing £100

Key terms

Indirect tax A tax on spending, sometimes used to reduce consumption of demerit goods.

Subsidy A payment made to producers to encourage increased production of a good or service.

Advantages of using indirect taxation	Disadvantages of using indirect taxation
▪ Revenues for governments can be hypothecated to specific areas of spending ▪ Use of the price mechanism leaves it up to consumers and producers to decide how to adjust their behaviour ▪ Helps to internalise external costs	▪ If placed on inelastic goods, the quantity demanded may not fall much unless the tax is very large ▪ Difficult to place an accurate value on external costs, which makes it hard to correctly 'internalise' a negative externality ▪ Tend to be regressive, meaning they take a larger percentage of a poorer person's income ▪ May reduce international competitiveness of UK firms

Subsidies

- Government grants paid to producers to encourage increased production of certain goods or services, such as merit goods.
- Can also be used to promote the use of products which reduce external costs, such as public transport.
- Granting a government subsidy has the effect of shifting the supply curve to the right.

Advantages of using subsidies	Disadvantages of using subsidies
▪ Can increase consumption of merit goods ▪ Reduce the price of a good, making it more affordable for those on lower incomes, reducing relative poverty	▪ Difficult to place an accurate monetary value on the size of external benefits ▪ Funding carries an opportunity cost ▪ Firms may become reliant on subsidies, encouraging productive inefficiency and laziness, reducing international competitiveness ▪ May be viewed by foreign governments as a form of artificial trade protection, encouraging them to retaliate ▪ If placed on goods or services with inelastic demand, they may reduce price but not significantly increase consumption

Minimum prices

- Price floors which establish a legal level below which prices are not allowed to fall, e.g. national minimum wage.
- The impact of a minimum price is shown in Figure 53.
- A minimum price (P_1) set above the free market price (P^*) for a good will create excess supply, equal to $Q_S - Q_D$, as shown in Figure 53.

Key terms

Minimum price A price floor placed above the free market equilibrium price.

Maximum price A price ceiling placed below the free market equilibrium price.

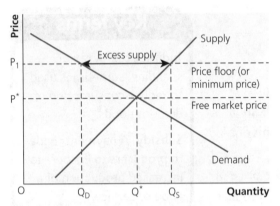

Figure 53 The effect of a minimum price

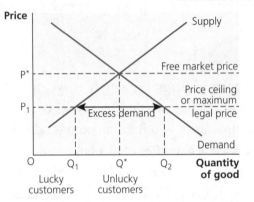

Figure 54 The effect of a maximum price

Advantages of minimum prices	Disadvantages of minimum prices
<ul><li>Give producers a guaranteed minimum price and income, which helps to generate a reasonable standard of living</li><li>Encourage production of essential products, e.g. agriculture</li><li>Excess supplies may be bought up and stored, to be released in times of future shortage</li></ul>	<ul><li>Higher price reduces disposable incomes</li><li>Encourage over-production and inefficiency</li><li>Opportunity costs if governments or other authorities have to purchase excess supplies</li><li>Reduced international competitiveness</li><li>May encourage people to seek cheaper, potentially more harmful alternatives</li></ul>

Maximum prices

- A price ceiling above which prices are not permitted to rise.
- Free market equilibrium price would be too high for many consumers, leading to problems of reduced affordability, e.g. rent controls to make accommodation more affordable.
- The impact of a maximum price is shown in Figure 54.
- A maximum price (P_1) set below the free market price (P^*) for a good will create excess demand, equal to $Q_2 - Q_1$, as shown as shown in Figure 54.

Exam tips

- Practise drawing accurate minimum and maximum price diagrams and illustrate how they may lead to excess supply and excess demand respectively.
- Make sure you don't get maximum price and minimum price the wrong way around. Remember, a maximum price is intended to stop prices rising too high; a minimum price is intended to stop prices falling too low. This distinction is often tested in multiple-choice questions.

Advantages of maximum prices	Disadvantages of maximum prices
■ Some people would otherwise not be able to afford certain goods and services, e.g. prescription medications ■ Can reduce the ability of firms with monopoly power to exploit consumers through charging higher prices	■ Creation of excess demand: queues, shortages and waiting lists ■ May lead to black markets for goods and services, e.g. secondary markets for music event tickets

Direct provision

- A government may decide provision cannot be left to the free market, since the good or service may be provided in either insufficient or excessive quantities (in the case of merit and demerit goods) or not at all (in the case of public goods).
- The government will organise provision of the product in question, then fund it out of tax revenue.
- Governments may pay a private sector firm to wholly or partially produce the good or service, e.g. paying a construction firm to build a new school.
- Goods or services may be free or nearly free 'at the point of consumption', so individuals do not have to worry about making a payment when they attend state school or require medical treatment.

Regulation

- Rules or laws to control or restrict the actions of economic agents in order to reduce market failure.
- Examples include:
  - □ banning smoking in public places
  - □ imposing maximum emissions levels on new cars
  - □ setting up regulatory bodies (such as OFGEM) to restrict the activities of dominant firms
- If firms or consumers do not obey the rules and laws they may be punished, e.g. with fines, limitations on trading activities, or even imprisonment.

> **Key term**
>
> **Regulation** Rules or laws used to control or restrict the actions of economic agents in order to reduce market failure.

Correcting information failure

- Governments may intervene in markets where there is too much or too little consumption of particular goods or services, e.g. because of a lack of information about the effects of consumption and production, such as in the case of merit and demerit goods.
- Methods to remedy information failure include:
  - □ compulsory labelling on food, along with 'traffic-lighting' levels of fat, salt etc.

☐ strong health warnings on packs of cigarettes

☐ television advertising campaigns discouraging excessive alcohol consumption

■ Drawbacks include high costs and a lack of long-term effectiveness.

Extending property rights and the use of pollution permits

■ A key reason for over-exploitation of natural resources such as oceans, forests and the atmosphere is a lack of clearly defined property rights or ownership of these resources.

■ **Pollution permits** are legal rights to use or exploit economic resources to a specific degree, e.g. fishing permits and CO_2 pollution permits.

■ Pollution permits can be presented and analysed using a diagram, as in Figure 55.

■ A regulating organisation such as a government will set a fixed supply of permits, such as S_{2016}, leading to a market price of P_{2016}.

■ It can reduce supply over time, e.g. to S_{2020} in order to strengthen incentives for firms to reduce emissions.

Key term

Pollution permit The right to use or exploit an economic resource to a specific degree, e.g. a fishing permit or permits to release CO_2 into the atmosphere.

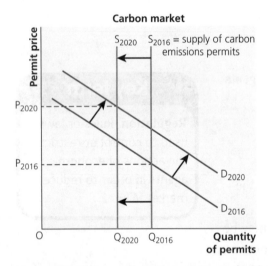

Figure 55 Using pollution permits to tackle environmental market failure

Advantages of pollution permits	Disadvantages of pollution permits
■ Use the market mechanism to provide powerful incentives for firms to reduce their carbon emissions ■ Revenues from selling permits can be used to fund 'green' technologies and other environmental schemes	■ Governments will suffer from imperfect information about the full social costs of CO_2 emissions, which may lead to government failure in deciding the quantity of permits to set ■ If the price of permits is set too low, firms will not be sufficiently incentivised to cut their CO_2 emissions

Competition policy

- Measures to enhance competition between firms in order to improve economic outcomes for society, e.g. legislation, privatisation, deregulation, prevention of mergers and various actions to prevent restrictive trade practices and abuse of monopoly power.
- UK **competition policy** is currently overseen by the Competition and Markets Authority (CMA).

Principles of UK competition policy

- In the UK, the CMA is the government agency responsible for overseeing competition policy.
- Main theoretical principles include:
  - □ ignoring economies of scale, perfect competition is more likely to be productively and allocatively efficient than monopoly
  - □ monopolists restrict output to raise price and gain supernormal profit, resulting in a net loss of welfare
  - □ if economies of scale are present, monopolies may produce output at a lower average total cost than firms in perfect competition
  - □ monopoly firms making supernormal profit can be more dynamically efficient than firms in perfect competition
  - □ in general, each case is judged on its own merits
- Competition policy in the UK is focused on four areas:
  - □ monopolies
  - □ mergers
  - □ restrictive trading practices
  - □ promoting competition

Monopolies

- The CMA uses a structure, conduct and performance approach to judging the relative merits of each investigation it makes.
- Possible approaches to tackling monopolies include:
  - □ compulsory break-up
  - □ windfall taxes on 'excess' or supernormal profits
  - □ price controls such as maximum prices
  - □ public ownership (nationalisation)
  - □ privatisation
  - □ deregulation

Mergers

- When two or more firms willingly join together.
- Competition policy considers whether **mergers** and **takeovers** might create a new monopoly.

> **Exam tip**
>
> Detailed knowledge of UK and EU competition law is *not* required.

> **Key term**
>
> **Competition policy**
> Government policy which aims to make markets more competitive.

> **Key terms**
>
> **Merger** When two or more firms willingly join together.
>
> **Takeover** When two or more firms unwillingly join together.

■ Mergers and takeovers may be prohibited if they are predicted to substantially reduce competition.

Restrictive trading practices

■ These include:
  □ forming a cartel to fix the price of a good or service
  □ refusal to supply a specific retailer
  □ 'full-line forcing' — obliging a retailer to stock all products in the firm's current range
  □ charging discriminatory prices, e.g. discounts for bulk orders
■ The CMA will usually require the firm(s) involved to stop the practice under threat of prosecution.

Public ownership, privatisation, regulation and deregulation of markets

Public ownership

■ **Public ownership** is when firms, industries or other assets are owned by government.
■ Advantages include:
  □ **nationalised** monopolies are more likely to take account of externalities
  □ state-run monopolies are more likely to produce an allocatively efficient output
  □ key industries such as rail, energy, steel and water may be regarded as too important to be run by private organisations
■ Disadvantages include:
  □ lack of dynamic efficiency
  □ the best managers and leaders are to be found in the private sector, where financial rewards may be significantly higher

> ### Key terms
>
> **Public ownership** Government ownership of firms, industries or other assets.
>
> **Nationalisation** The transfer of assets from the private sector to public ownership.
>
> **Privatisation** The sale of government-owned assets to the private sector.

Privatisation

Advantages of privatisation	Disadvantages of privatisation
■ Raising extra revenue for the government ■ Promoting competition ■ Promoting efficiency ■ Encouraging greater share ownership by the general public may lead to greater pressure on firms to act in the public interest	■ Exploitation of monopoly power ■ Short-termism: a focus on cost-cutting to maximise short-term profits rather than on longer-term investment projects ■ Private firms may ignore the externalities of their activities

Regulation

- Rules and laws which restrict market freedom.
- External regulation involves agencies such as the CMA imposing rules and restrictions.
- Self-regulation involves organisations in particular industries voluntarily regulating themselves, e.g. membership of a professional governing body such as the Institute of Chartered Accountants in England and Wales, or the Law Society.
- While regulation may impose additional costs on businesses, it is felt to be justified in protecting consumers from abuse of monopoly power and external costs.
- However, regulation may lead to the problem of regulatory capture.

Deregulation

- The removal of rules and regulations in order to increase the efficiency of markets.
- May reduce firms' costs of production, meaning consumers benefit from lower prices.
- The promotion of competition may lead to a more contestable market.
- May avoid the problem of regulatory capture.

Government failure

Government failure is when government intervention in a market leads to a misallocation of resources.

Reasons for government failure:

- inadequate information
- unintended consequences
- market distortions
- administrative costs
- regulatory capture

Key terms

Regulation The imposition of rules and laws which restrict market freedom.

Regulatory capture When the regulatory bodies (such as OFGEM in the case of gas and electricity suppliers) set up to oversee the behaviour of privatised monopolies come to be unduly influenced by the firms they have been set up to monitor.

Deregulation The removal of rules and regulations in order to increase the efficiency of markets.

Government failure When government intervention in a market reduces overall economic welfare.

Synoptic link

Competition policy, privatisation and deregulation may be considered aspects of supply-side policy used to improve the efficiency of markets.

Do you know?

1 State the two key characteristics of a public good.
2 Using a diagram in each case, illustrate positive externalities in production, positive externalities in consumption, negative externalities in production and negative externalities in consumption.
3 Explain three reasons for the under-consumption of merit goods.
4 Explain two advantages and two disadvantages of using indirect taxation to tackle environmental market failure.
5 Explain three policies that could be used to control the actions of monopolies in the UK.

End of section 1 questions

1 Define the term 'rational consumer'.

2 Define the term 'normal good'.

3 Define the term 'specialisation'.

4 Define the term 'price discrimination'.

5 Define the term 'government failure'.

6 With the help of a PPC diagram, illustrate and explain the opportunity cost situation facing governments with regard to public spending on roads versus schools.

7 With the help of a diagram, explain how mandating choices towards saving for pensions might influence the market towards more desirable outcomes.

8 With the help of a diagram, explain how imperfect information surrounding education could lead to under-consumption in a free market.

9 Explain three reasons why some groups of workers may earn more than others.

10 Explain why a firm's costs of production may be influenced by diminishing returns in the short run and increasing returns to scale in the long run.

11 Explain why firms in perfectly competitive markets may be productively and allocatively efficient.

12 Explain three possible benefits of privatisation of industries such as rail or the postal service.

13 Analyse how immobility of labour may lead to an inequitable distribution of income and wealth.

14 Evaluate the view that the best way to increase wage rates and levels of employment in any labour market is to increase membership of trade unions.

15 Evaluate policy measures the government could use to increase competition in industries such as transport, supermarkets and banking.

16 Evaluate alternative methods that could be used to tackle market failure, such as too much household waste.

17 Evaluate methods that could be used to encourage individuals to lead a healthier lifestyle.

2 National and international economy

2.1 Measuring economic performance

You need to know
- objectives of government economic policy
- conflicts arising when attempting to achieve economic objectives
- economic indicators used to measure economic performance
- what index numbers are and how they measure changes in the price level
- uses and limitations of national income data

Objectives of government economic policy

Main economic objectives

- Governments attempt to influence **macroeconomic** performance to achieve **economic objectives** for the economy.
- **Economic policies** are the tools used by the government to achieve these objectives.

The main economic objectives are:
- **economic growth**
- price stability
- minimising **unemployment**
- stable balance of payments on current account
- balancing the **budget**
- achieving an equitable **distribution of income**

Conflict in achieving economic objectives

- Achieving all economic objectives simultaneously is difficult — there are **policy conflicts**.

- A **trade-off** can occur. Policy conflicts are more likely to occur in the short run.
- In the long run, it may be possible to achieve all of the objectives at the same time.
- Policy conflicts can be avoided by using different policies to achieve different objectives.

Importance of economic objectives

The most important government economic objectives are likely to be:
- achieving economic growth
- achieving price stability
- minimising unemployment

Their importance changes over time, e.g.:
- In the 1970s, very high inflation meant achieving price stability was a higher priority.
- Following the 2008 financial crisis, achieving economic growth became more important than achieving price stability.

Other objectives gain importance at certain times:
- Recently, the UK government placed a higher priority on the elimination of the budget deficit.

Macroeconomic indicators

- **Real gross domestic product (GDP)**: real GDP has been adjusted for changes in the price level over the same period.
- **Real GDP per capita**: GDP per capita shows average income earned by each member of the population. This has been adjusted for changes in the price level:

$$\text{real GDP per capita} = \frac{\text{real GDP in total (£s)}}{\text{population level (millions)}}$$

- **Consumer price index (CPI)**: this shows the average level of prices of a typical basket of goods and services. CPI is the price index used by the government to calculate the official rate of price inflation.
- **Retail price index (RPI)**: RPI is an alternative price index used which shows the average level of prices of a typical basket of goods and services.
- **Measures of unemployment**: there are two main measures of unemployment used in the UK:
  - □ **Claimant count** includes those receiving benefit payments for being unemployed.
  - □ The **labour force survey** includes all those looking for but unable to find work, whether or not they're receiving benefit payments.

Key terms

Trade-off The opportunity cost in terms of moving further away from achieving one objective in the process of moving closer to achieving another objective.

Macroeconomic indicators Economic variables showing how well the government is doing in achieving its economic objectives.

Gross domestic product (GDP) A measure of national income showing the value of output produced in an economy for a period (usually 1 year).

Synoptic link

Achieving an equitable distribution of income is based on a value judgement — it is difficult to quantify the exact 'best' distribution of income.

Exam tip

When writing extended answers in macroeconomics, the difference between the short run and the long run isn't fixed. However, the short run is often taken to mean within the next year or two. The long run is beyond the period of 1–2 years.

- Productivity:

$$\text{labour productivity} = \frac{\text{output (in units)}}{\text{number of workers or worker hours}}$$

$$\text{capital productivity} = \frac{\text{output (in units)}}{\text{value of capital equipment (£s)}}$$

- **Balance of payments** on **current account**: The current account is part of the balance of payments, including trade in goods and services as well as net flows of income related to overseas investments. It is balanced when the inflows of money match the outflows of money.

Uses of index numbers

- Index numbers start with a base year value — normally 100.
- Changes in the variable are measured by how far they move away from the base year value, e.g.:
  - ☐ GDP is £2000 billion in the base year and rises to £2200 in year 2.
  - ☐ The base year index number for GDP is 100. The index for GDP in year 2 is therefore 110 (a 10% rise in its value).
- Index numbers are useful for:
  - ☐ Showing changes in data (such as GDP or the price level) when it is the change that matters and not the actual size of the variables.
  - ☐ Comparing multiple variables when it is the changes that matter rather than the size of the variables (e.g. making comparisons over time for different countries).

Index numbers and the price level

- The price level is the average level of prices at a point in time — represented as an index number.
- The CPI and RPI use index numbers to show the price level.
- RPI includes mortgage interest payments in its calculations (CPI does not).
- Inflation is the percentage change in the price level, e.g. if CPI increases from 100 to 103 over 1 year, the inflation rate is 3%.
- The CPI calculates an average level of prices based on prices for a range of goods and services. This is known as a **basket of goods and services**.
- The basket of goods and services is meant to represent the spending patterns and prices paid by a typical UK household.
- The CPI is a **weighted average**. Goods and services that households spend more of their income on (e.g. food and transport) are given a higher weighting.

Key terms

Productivity The quantity of output produced by a given level of inputs (labour or capital equipment) for a given period.

Balance of payments A financial record of all transactions between the UK and the rest of the world.

Current account A record of the trade in goods and services and flows of income between the UK and the rest of the world.

Basket of goods and services A range of goods and services bought by the typical household.

Weighted average Items that account for a larger proportion of a household budget are given a higher weighting in the price indices used in the UK.

Uses of national income data

Exam tip

Make sure you are comparing per capita measures of GDP when making judgements about living standards.

- Real GDP shows what GDP can 'buy' after adjusting for changes in prices over time.
- This measure of GDP is used to assess the standard of living of a country's population:

$$\text{real GDP per capita} = \frac{\text{real GDP in (£s)}}{\text{population}}$$

- A higher GDP per capita means individuals can buy more, increasing the population's standard of living.

Other uses of national income data

- Determine economic growth
- Estimate likely tax revenues
- Estimate likely welfare expenditure (such as unemployment benefits)
- Assess inflationary pressure (if national income is rising rapidly)

Limitations of national income data

These include:

- **distribution of income**
  - ☐ looks at how income is shared out
  - ☐ a country with high income inequality has more people with incomes significantly below the average GDP per capita than one with a more equal distribution of income
  - ☐ high levels of income inequality make GDP per capita less reliable in measuring living standards
- **composition of GDP**
  - ☐ military spending (which directly benefits few people) can be a significant percentage of GDP
  - ☐ some contributions to GDP (e.g. spending on health and education) increase the living standards more than other contributions
- shadow economy
  - ☐ incomes from legal but unrecorded transactions (often to avoid tax charges)
  - ☐ transactions which are both illegal and unrecorded, e.g. drugs or prostitution
  - ☐ unrecorded transactions add to the living standards of the population but do not show in official GDP data
  - ☐ failure to include the shadow economy understates living standards
  - ☐ estimates suggest the UK's shadow economy is worth 10% of actual GDP

Exam tip

Although there are weaknesses in using GDP per capita to determine living standards, the statistic is still a useful guide and should not be dismissed.

Key term

Shadow economy The value of transactions not recorded in official national income statistics.

- **non-marketed output**
  - ☐ many goods and services add to people's standard of living but do not show up in official GDP data
  - ☐ services such as DIY and childcare are not included in the GDP if performed by other family members for free — but these add significantly to welfare and living standards. Only paid-for services are recorded in GDP
- **negative externalities**
  - ☐ additions to GDP often generate negative externalities, reducing living standards
  - ☐ pollution and traffic congestion usually arise out of increased activity but reduce people's quality of life
  - ☐ therefore, increases in GDP often overstate improvements to people's standard of living
- **non-financial factors**
  - ☐ quality of health provision and whether it is free to use
  - ☐ education provision, in terms of length and quality
  - ☐ individual freedom, e.g. of speech and travel
  - ☐ the amount of leisure time enjoyed on average, e.g. number of public holidays and limits on hours worked per week

Purchasing power parity (PPP)

- Making comparisons of living standards between countries requires conversion of GDP into common currency.
- Using **purchasing power parity** exchange rates avoids the problem of using inappropriate exchange rates, e.g. that are volatile or under- or over-valued.
- The PPP exchange rate is the rate where goods and services in different countries would be the same price once converted into common currencies.
- A problem with this approach is that it assumes the goods being compared in price are identical, which is unlikely to be the case.

GDP data and living standards

- GDP per capita is not a perfect measure of living standards, but is commonly used.
- Adjustments can be made (e.g. correcting for wide income inequality), but GDP remains an easy-to-understand, widely used measure.
- Other measurements are used, such as the Human Development Index (HDI), but are not widely understood or accepted.

Do you know?

1 State the government's main macroeconomic objectives.
2 Identify and explain two possible conflicts between macroeconomic objectives.
3 State what is meant by a price index.

2.2 How the macroeconomy works

You need to know

■ how the circular flow of income model works
■ what national income measures
■ how aggregate demand (AD) is measured and determined
■ how short-run, long-run and Keynesian aggregate supply (AS) is measured and determined
■ how to calculate the size of the multiplier effect
■ how macroeconomic equilibrium is determined
■ how the economy is affected by demand and supply shocks

Circular flow of income

National income is measured by three methods:

■ income method
■ output method
■ expenditure method

Each method gives the same value.

national income = national output = national expenditure

Real national income

■ Increases in national income are separated into **real** and **nominal** increases.

$$\text{real GDP} = \text{nominal GDP} \times \left(\frac{\text{price level in previous year}}{\text{price level in current year}}\right)$$

Example:

■ If nominal GDP increases from £2000 to £2200 billion and the price level has risen from 114 to 120 over the same period, then:

$$\text{real GDP is } £2200 \text{ billion} \times \left(\frac{114}{120}\right) = £2090 \text{ billion}$$

$$\text{real economic growth is } \left(\frac{£2090\text{bn} - £2000\text{bn}}{£2090\text{bn}}\right) \times 100 = 4.5\%$$

Key terms

Real national income National income adjusted to take into account inflation.

Nominal income National income unadjusted for price changes.

The circular flow of income model

- Income and expenditure are monetary flows circulating around the economy:
  - ☐ money flows from households to firms as expenditure
  - ☐ money flows back from firms to households as incomes
- Injections add money into the circular flow:
  - ☐ investment (I)
  - ☐ government expenditure (G)
  - ☐ exports (X)
- Withdrawals take money out of the circular flow:
  - ☐ savings (S)
  - ☐ taxation (T)
  - ☐ imports (M)

The full circular flow model is shown in Figure 56.

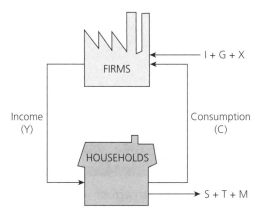

Figure 56 The full model of the circular flow of income, with money withdrawn in the form of savings and injected back into the flow in the form of investment

- Macroeconomic equilibrium is where total injections = total withdrawals.
  - ☐ If injections > withdrawals: national income increases.
  - ☐ If injections < withdrawals: national income decreases.

Aggregate demand

Determinants of aggregate demand

- Consumption (C) by households
- Investment (I) by businesses
- Government expenditure (G)
- Net exports (exports (X) – imports (M)) by UK and foreign consumers/producers
- The formula is:
  $$AD = C + I + G + X - M$$

Key terms

Circular flow of income A model of the economy showing flows of income and expenditure.

Injection Money entering the circular flow from governments, businesses or the foreign sector.

Withdrawals Money leaving the circular flow, either for savings, taxation or spending on imports.

Aggregate demand (AD) Total planned expenditure at any given price level (C + G + I + X – M).

Consumption Spending by households on consumer goods and services.

Exam tip

The components of AD are not equally sized. Consumption accounts for over two-thirds of AD, so changes in this matter more than, say, changes in exports when looking at the effects of a change in AD.

■ The aggregate demand (AD) curve shows the relationship between AD (total expenditure) and the price level in an economy. It shifts if any component of AD increases (rightward shift) or decreases (leftward shift), as shown in Figure 57.

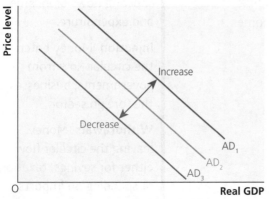

Figure 57 Aggregate demand (AD) showing the amounts of planned expenditure that would occur at different price levels

Determinants of consumption

■ Income (higher income means higher consumption)
■ Interest rates:
  □ higher interest rates encourage saving — and vice versa
  □ higher interest rates reduce credit-financed consumption — and vice versa
  □ higher interest rates mean higher mortgage repayments so less available to spend — and vice versa
■ Consumer confidence
■ Taxation (on incomes)
■ Wealth effect
■ Unemployment

Determinants of saving

■ income
■ interest rates
■ tax (on interest received from saving)
■ consumer confidence
■ government regulation (e.g. contractual savings, such as pension contributions)

Determinants of investment

■ Interest rates
■ Business confidence
■ Tax (on profits)
■ Advances in technology

The accelerator process

Investment is affected by changes in national income.

- The accelerator process is where changes in national income will lead to greater changes in the level of investment.
- Increases in national income generate more investment as businesses expand their productive capacity.

Determinants of government expenditure and net exports

Government spending affects AD and the ability to achieve economic objectives.

- Increases in government spending boost economic growth and reduce unemployment.
- Decreases in government spending reduce inflation.

Factors affecting government spending are covered in Section 2.5. See Section 2.6 for determinants of exports and imports (net exports).

The multiplier process

- Changes in AD normally lead to larger than proportional changes explains in real GDP because of the **multiplier process**.
- The multiplier process explains how changes in spending lead to changes in income, leading to further changes in spending and so on.
  - ☐ For example, if an increase in injections of £200 m leads to an increase in national income of £600 m, then the size of the multiplier is £600 m/£200 m = 3.
- The size of the multiplier is affected by the marginal propensity to consume (MPC).
- The multiplier is calculated as follows:

$$\frac{1}{(1 - \text{MPC})}$$

- The multiplier can work in a positive or negative way — increasing or decreasing national income.
- If the MPC increases, then the size of the multiplier increases.
- If the MPC decreases, the size of the multiplier decreases.
  - ☐ For example, if the MPC is 0.75 (i.e. 75% of any additional income is consumed) then the size of the multiplier would be:

$$\frac{1}{(1 - 0.75)} = 4$$

  - ☐ If the MPC falls to 0.6, the size of the multiplier falls to:

$$\frac{1}{(1 - 0.6)} = 2.5$$

Aggregate supply

Short-run aggregate supply (SRAS)

Determinants of SRAS

- wage rates
- other input costs
- indirect taxes
- exchange rate
- productivity

Shifts in the SRAS curve

- If any determinant of SRAS changes, the SRAS curve shifts leftwards or rightwards (Figure 58).
  - ☐ Increases in production costs reduce the profitability of production — SRAS curve shifts leftwards ($SRAS_1$ TO $SRAS_2$).
  - ☐ Decreases in production costs increase the profitability of production — SRAS curve shifts rightwards ($SRAS_1$ TO $SRAS_3$).
- Movements along the SRAS curve occur when there is a shift in AD.

Long-run aggregate supply (LRAS)

- Long-run aggregate supply (LRAS) shows the level of output if the economy is operating at its *full* capacity level.
- The LRAS curve is vertical, meaning the capacity level of output is the same at all price levels (i.e. it is fixed).
- Increases in full capacity output are achieved through long-run changes to the economy, as shown in Figure 59 by $LRAS_1$ shifting to $LRAS_2$.

Determinants of LRAS

- quantity and quality of factors of production
- technology
- productivity
- factor mobility
- enterprise
- economic incentives and attitudes
- supply-side policies

Institutional structure of the economy

- LRAS is affected by the institutional structure of the economy, e.g. the legal and financial systems.

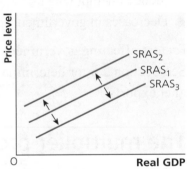

Figure 58 Shifts in the SRAS curve

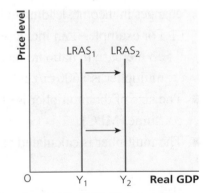

Figure 59 Shifts in a vertical LRAS curve

- Ensuring the institutional structure works efficiently and fairly helps increase LRAS.
- After the 2008 financial crisis, the UK government intervened to help banks continue lending money to businesses.

The Keynesian AS curve

- An alternative AS curve to the SRAS and LRAS is the Keynesian AS curve (Figure 60).
- No distinction is made between short-run and long-run AS curves.
- At low levels, real GDP can be increased with no upward pressure on prices.
- As the economy gets close to capacity level, prices begin rising — in Figure 60, the AS curve begins to slope upwards.
- The AS curve is perfectly inelastic at the full capacity output, and increases in AD lead to higher price levels.

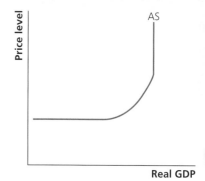

Figure 60 The Keynesian AS curve

Macroeconomic equilibrium

Short-run equilibrium

- Short-run macroeconomic equilibrium — measured by the price level and real GDP level — is determined by interaction between SRAS and AD.
- Any change in AD or SRAS changes the equilibrium position.
  - □ An increase in AD increases both real GDP and the price level, shown in Figure 61 by the shift from AD_1 to AD_2.
  - □ A decrease in SRAS decreases real GDP but increases the price level, shown in Figure 62 by the shift from $SRAS_1$ to $SRAS_2$.

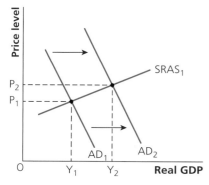

Figure 61 The effect of an increase in AD

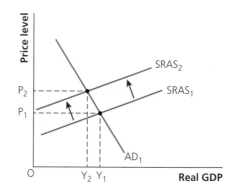

Figure 62 The effect of a decrease in SRAS

Long-run equilibrium

- Long-run equilibrium occurs where LRAS and AD intercept.
- The price level varies but the level of real GDP is constant.

- The long-run equilibrium level of real GDP is always at the full capacity output level (sometimes called **full employment output**).
- This is shown in Figure 63 where LRAS and AD intersect.

Economic shocks

- Shocks affect real GDP, unemployment and inflation.
- Shocks are either demand-side or supply-side (or both).

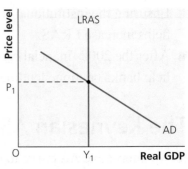

Figure 63 Long-run equilibrium

Demand-side shocks	Supply-side shocks
These affect AD	These affect LRAS
Examples include the 2008 financial crisis, a large fall in the exchange rate or an unexpectedly large change to interest rates	Examples include the massive oil price rises of the 1970s, a significant crop failure or a significant change to the price of an important commodity

Do you know?

1 If the MPC is 0.75, calculate the size of the multiplier.

2 Show, on an AD/AS diagram, the effects of an increase in consumer confidence.

3 Using an AS/AD diagram, explain the effects of increasing the retirement age in the UK.

4 Distinguish between the LRAS and the Keynesian AS curves.

5 Explain the impact of the financial crisis in 2008 on macroeconomic equilibrium.

Key terms

Demand-side shock An unexpected, sudden or large change to aggregate demand.

Supply-side shock An unexpected, sudden or large change to aggregate supply.

2.3 Economic performance

You need to know

- types of economic growth and the benefits and drawbacks of growth
- the economic cycle — its characteristics and explanations
- the causes and consequences of unemployment and the policies used to reduce it
- the causes and consequences of inflation and deflation and the policies used to target them
- how policy conflicts arise and are resolved, such as that shown on the Phillips curve

Economic growth

Short-run economic growth

- Caused by increases in AD and occurs when unemployed factors are brought into producing output.
- It can also be caused by increases in SRAS.
- It can be achieved through changes in government policy.
- Determinants of short-run growth include:
  - □ increases in any component of AD, shown by the increase from AD_1 to AD_2 in Figure 64
  - □ increases in any component of SRAS

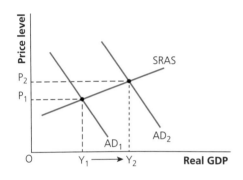

Figure 64 Increases in AD will produce short-run growth in the economy

Long-run economic growth

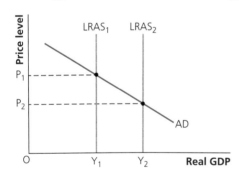

Figure 65 Shifts in the LRAS curve generate long-run growth

- Caused by increases in LRAS (i.e. increases in an economy's productive capacity), shown in Figure 65 by the rightward shift from $LRAS_1$ to $LRAS_2$.
- Long-run growth is also known as **trend growth**.
- Estimates of UK long-run growth are between 2% and 2.5% per year.
- Determinants of long-run growth include:
  - □ increases in the labour force (labour supply), such as:
    - encouraging participation from the **economically inactive**
    - decreasing the attractiveness of remaining unemployed
    - increasing the retirement age/decreasing the school leaving age
    - encouraging immigration/discouraging emigration

☐ improving labour productivity

☐ new technology

☐ education — improving productivity or occupational mobility

☐ government policy — supply-side policies (see Section 2.5)

Short-run and long-run growth can be shown using production possibility curves (PPC, Figure 66):

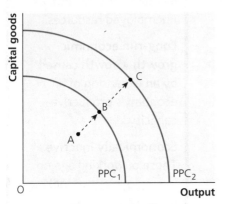

Figure 66 **Short-run and long-run economic growth**

Synoptic link

There is a link between short-run and long-run growth and the factors that affect the shape of the PPC and the position within (or on) the PPC, covered in Section 1.1.

■ Short-run growth is the movement within a PPC (shown as the movement from A to B).

■ Long-run growth is the outward shift of the PPC (i.e. shown by the movement from B to C).

Costs and benefits of economic growth

Economic growth has effects on:

■ individuals   ■ economies   ■ the environment

Benefits	Costs
■ Higher living standards	■ Increases in negative externalities
■ Easier to find jobs	
■ Social indicator improvements	■ Potential increases in inequality
■ Increase tax revenue	■ Natural resource depletion
■ Lower welfare expenditure	■ Increases in inflation
■ Lower absolute poverty (another government objective)	
■ Status and prestige for the government	

Synoptic link

There is a link between the costs of economic growth and market failure caused by externalities covered in Section 1.8.

Environmental impact of growth

■ Sustainable growth may avoid some of the negative costs of economic growth.

■ Governments can encourage sustainable growth through taxes, subsidies and regulation.

The economic cycle

Phases of the economic cycle

There are four stages of the **economic cycle**, as shown in Figure 67.

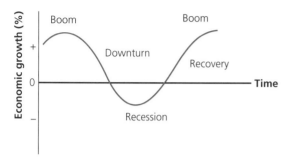

Figure 67 The economic cycle

Key terms

Economic cycle The repeated fluctuations in short-term growth over time.

Trend growth The expansion of the economy's productive capacity over time.

Output gap The difference between actual growth and trend growth.

Boom	Downturn	Recession	Recovery
Above average economic growth	Economic growth falls (but still positive)	Economic growth is very low or negative	Economic growth is positive but below average
Unemployment falls, reaching low levels	Unemployment stops falling (but may not rise yet due to labour hoarding)	Unemployment rises quickly, reaching high levels	Unemployment remains high but may stop rising
Inflation rises as economy 'overheats'	Inflation is high but stops rising	Inflation falls, reaching low levels (with possible deflation)	Inflation remains low but stops falling
High consumer/business confidence	Consumer/business confidence falls	Low consumer/business confidence	Consumer/business confidence is low but begins rising
Budget balance moves into surplus/smaller deficit	Budget balance moves towards/further into deficit	Budget balance moves further into deficit	Budget balance remains in deficit but deficit will not increase
Current account balance moves into deficit/deficit increases	Current account balance moves towards surplus/smaller deficit	Current account balance moves towards/into surplus	Current account balance remains in surplus but does not grow/may begin to move into deficit

Output gaps

Actual growth diverges from **trend growth**, resulting in **output gaps**. These can be positive or negative, as shown in Figure 68.

Exam tip

The length of each stage of the economic cycle is not fixed and can vary.

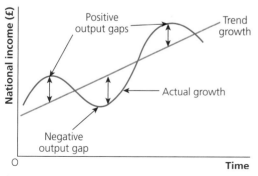

Figure 68 Output gaps exist when short-run growth deviates from long-run or trend growth

Answers at **www.hoddereducation.co.uk/needtoknow/answers**

Positive output gap: actual growth > trend growth	Negative output gap: actual growth < trend growth
Unemployment probably falling	Unemployment probably rising
Inflation probably rising	Inflation probably falling

Explanations of the economic cycle

- multiplier–accelerator model
- inventory cycle
- asset price bubbles
- herding
- excessive growth in credit
- economic shocks

Employment and unemployment

- Full employment refers to the lowest level of unemployment practically achievable.
- Unemployment in the UK is measured by:
  - ☐ claimant count
  - ☐ labour force survey

Types of unemployment

Appropriate policies to reduce unemployment depend on the type (or cause) of unemployment, as illustrated in the table below.

	Seasonal unemployment	Cyclical unemployment	Frictional unemployment	Structural unemployment
Cause	Seasonal decline in demand for output of seasonal industries	Insufficient AD	People moving into and out of employment	Geographical immobility (regional unemployment) Occupational immobility Global factors — competition from low-cost producers overseas
Policy to reduce	This is not a major concern of the government	Boost AD with: ■ lower interest rates ■ lower taxes ■ higher government spending	Improving information about job vacancies Ensuring the welfare system does not create incentives to remain unemployed	Supply-side policies

Demand and supply-side factors

- Unemployment is also caused by demand-side and supply-side factors:

□ demand-side factors — by low aggregate demand (**cyclical unemployment**)

□ supply-side factors — by issues of long-run aggregate supply (e.g. **frictional** and **structural** factors).

■ Governments use a range of policies to affect both demand-side and supply-side causes.

Voluntary and involuntary unemployment

Voluntary unemployment	Involuntary unemployment
Workers choose not to accept work at the going wage rate (frictional unemployment may be **voluntary**)	Workers cannot find work at the going wage rate (cyclical unemployment) Structural unemployment may be voluntary or **involuntary** and depends on value judgements made by economists

Real wage unemployment

■ **Real wage unemployment** occurs when real wages exceed the free market wage rate and cannot fall to restore labour market equilibrium. This is shown in Figure 69, where the wage rate of W_2 leads to the employment level falling to Q_2.

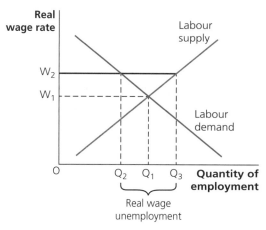

Figure 69 Real wage unemployment caused by the failure of the labour market to 'clear'

■ Real wage unemployment can be caused by:
□ high minimum wages
□ trade unions pushing wages up
□ wages being sticky downwards (i.e. difficulties for businesses in cutting wages).

The natural rate of unemployment

■ Unemployment stills exist even with labour market equilibrium.
■ The **natural rate of unemployment** is also referred to as **full employment**.

- It is where no cyclical unemployment exists.
- The natural rate of unemployment is the vertical portion of the AS curve (either on a Keynesian AS curve or an LRAS curve)
- It consists of voluntary, frictional and structural factors.

Frictional factors

- These occur when:
  - □ unemployment benefits are too high
  - □ replacement ratio is too high (replacement ratio > 1 means income from being unemployed is greater than income from employment)

$$\text{replacement ratio} = \frac{\text{out of work disposable income}}{\text{in work disposable income}}$$

- Replacement ratio can be lowered by:
  - □ less generous unemployment benefits
  - □ minimum wage increases
  - □ tax credits (allowing people in work to keep some of their benefit payments)

Structural factors

- Regional unemployment exists if people are unwilling/unable to move to job vacancies. This can be due to:
  - □ lack of knowledge of vacancies
  - □ difficulties accessing housing in expensive areas
  - □ family ties
  - □ poor transport links
- People may need training in new skills before they are able to accept job vacancies:
  - □ declining industries required different skills from new, growing industries
  - □ training takes time to arrange and may not be sufficiently provided to ensure people obtain the necessary training to fill vacancies

Voluntary factors

- People may 'choose' to be voluntarily unemployed.

The natural rate of unemployment can be reduced through creating policies to reduce:

- voluntary unemployment
- frictional unemployment
- structural unemployment

> **Synoptic link**
>
> Structural unemployment is viewed as a form of market failure caused by factor immobility.

> **Exam tip**
>
> The cause of unemployment is not always obvious in reality. Current UK unemployment will have many causes and it is difficult to identify the exact proportions of each cause.

Consequences of unemployment

- individual ill-health
- family breakdown
- higher crime (this is disputed)
- economy doesn't operate on its PPC
- a larger budget deficit, due to
  - ☐ higher government expenditure on welfare
  - ☐ less tax revenue collected
- deskilling of working population (hysteresis)

Inflation and deflation

Causes of inflation

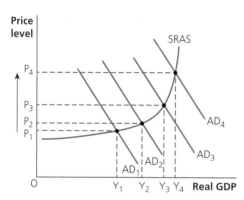

Figure 70 Growth in AD and its impact on demand-pull inflation

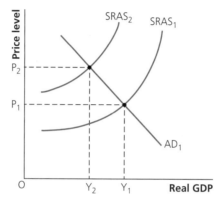

Figure 71 The impact of a leftward shift in SRAS

Demand-pull inflation	Cost-push inflation
Caused by excessive increases in AD, shown in Figure 71 as AD increases from AD_1 to AD_4 — each time leading to higher inflation Caused by AD rise above that needed to generate 'full employment' output	Caused by increases in production costs (i.e. decreases in SRAS or AS), as shown in Figure 71 by the leftward shift from $SRAS_1$ to $SRAS_2$ Increases in production costs are caused by increases in wages, material costs, power costs, and indirect taxes (e.g. VAT), and falls in the exchange rate (leading to 'imported inflation') Cost-push inflation is accompanied by falling GDP (and rising unemployment)
Can be reduced by: - Reducing government spending - Raising taxes - Raising interest rates	**Can be reduced by:** - Higher interest rates — leading to exchange rate rises - Improvements in labour market flexibility (e.g. reduction in trade union power)

Key term

Inflation Percentage change in the price level measured over a period of 1 year.

The quantity theory of money

- The quantity theory of money is based on the Fisher equation:

  $$MV = PQ$$

  where M = money supply, V = velocity of circulation (how fast money changes hands), P = price level, Q = real national output.
- If V is constant and Q grows at the trend rate of growth (assumed to be reasonably constant at around 2% per year), then any inflation is caused by money supply growth
- The quantity theory of money is an alternative explanation for inflation.
- It is favoured by monetarist economists.
- However, there are limitations:
  - □ V is not constant
  - □ M cannot be controlled easily due to the global nature of financial markets
  - □ Q doesn't grow at a constant rate over time
  - □ the causation doesn't necessarily flow from M to P (i.e. changes in M may not cause changes in P)
- The quantity theory of money was used in the late 1970s/early 1980s but has fallen out of favour since.

Consequences of inflation

- Menu costs
- Shoe leather/search costs
- Uncompetitive exports
- Fiscal drag — people may get pulled into higher tax bands
- Uncertainty
- Policy response — government is likely to raise interest rates if inflation rises

Expectations and changes in the price level

- The current rate of inflation is affected by people's expectations of future inflation.
- Expectations of inflation and actual inflation are connected through wage claims.
- People base wage claims on real wages and inflation expectations (e.g. for a real wage increase of 2% with inflation expected to be 3%, workers will push for a nominal wage increase of 5%).
- If people expect inflation to increase in the future, then they will ask for higher wage rates to compensate.

Deflation

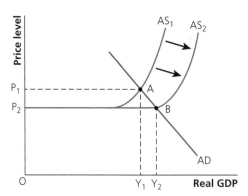

Figure 72 Benign deflation
— caused by increases in AS

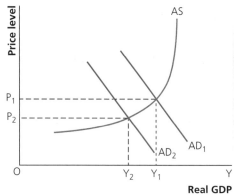

Figure 73 Malevolent deflation
— caused by falls in AD

Benign/good deflation	Malign/malevolent/bad deflation
Caused by increases in AS, shown in Figure 72 by the increase from AS_1 to AS_2	Caused by decreases in AD, shown in Figure 73 by the decrease from AD_1 to AD_2
Caused by advances in technology, falls in input prices (e.g. oil prices), rising productivity	Falls in AD leading to deflation are often the result of falling confidence and a demand-side shock
Leads to higher output and lower prices	Leads to lower output (and likely rises in unemployment) and lower prices

Consequences of deflation

- Delays in consumption — with falling prices, consumers may delay spending which can lead to a deflationary spiral.
- Rising real value of debt — debt is fixed in nominal terms and therefore increases in size relative to the income of borrowers if prices and incomes are falling.
- Sticky wages — businesses may try to cut wages to save money. Workers resist nominal wage cuts and this may lead to industrial conflict and possibly higher real wage unemployment.

Inflation targeting

- The UK inflation target is 2%, plus or minus 1% (i.e. 1–3%).
- High inflation causes economic problems.
- Deflation can be good or bad for an economy, depending on the type of deflation.
- Even good deflation can turn into bad deflation if it leads to falling AD.

Commodity prices and inflation

- Commodity prices are often volatile.
- Oil prices significantly affect the inflation rate due to oil's importance as a business input.

Key terms

Deflation A fall in the price level measured over a period of time.

Disinflation A fall in the rate of inflation.

Impact of other economies on UK inflation

- Growth overseas increases demand for UK exports and increases demand-pull inflation.
- Recession overseas decreases demand for UK exports and leads to lower demand-pull inflation.
- Increased growth overseas (especially in large economies such as China) may lead to rising commodity prices, which lead to cost-push inflation.
- Changes in overseas economies may lead to changes in the UK exchange rate, affecting cost-push pressures.

Exam tip

Cost-push inflation is more difficult to control than demand-pull inflation. Make sure you can explain how and why.

Possible conflicts between macroeconomic objectives

The Phillips curve

- The short-run Phillips curve (SRPC) shows the apparent trade-off between inflation and unemployment, as illustrated in Figure 74.
- As unemployment falls, trade unions have more power to push up wages — especially as labour shortages emerge.
- If wages rise, then inflation will also rise — the trade-off.
- To reduce inflation, AD is reduced and this leads to lower GDP and higher unemployment.
- This relationship broke down in the UK in the 1960s; both inflation and unemployment rose at same time — no trade-off!

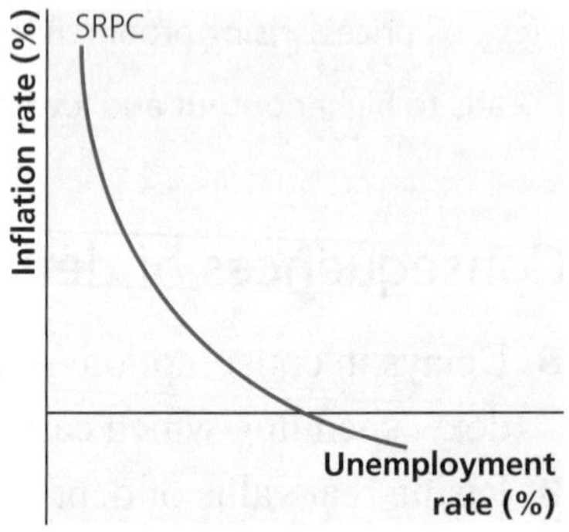

Figure 74 The short-run Phillips curve, showing the trade-off between unemployment and inflation

The long-run Phillips curve

- Unemployment/inflation trade-off only occurs in the short run.
- In the long run, unemployment rate returns to natural rate of unemployment.
  - □ As unemployment falls from U_1 to U_2 in Figure 75, the economy moves along $SRPC_1$ from A to B due to money illusion: workers have adaptive expectations and at B will ask for higher wages, since inflation has risen.
  - □ Rising wages mean firms reduce employment, and unemployment rises back to U_1.
  - □ Economy settles at point C — on a new SRPC where inflation expectations are now higher.

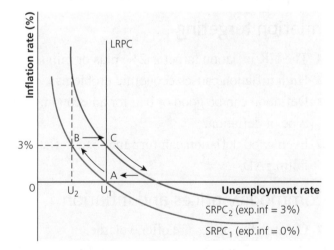

Figure 75 The long-run Phillips curve is vertical, at the natural rate of unemployment

- In the long run, Phillips curve is vertical at natural rate of unemployment.
- In the long run, unemployment is reduced only through policies lowering the natural rate of unemployment.
- NAIRU (non-accelerating inflation rate of unemployment) is often used instead of natural rate of unemployment.
- At NAIRU, inflation will neither rise nor fall.

Key term

NAIRU Non-accelerating inflation rate of unemployment (unemployment rate where inflation is constant).

Policy conflicts

- Reducing output gaps (positive and negative) may conflict in aiming for low unemployment and low inflation.
- Other policy conflicts exist:
  - □ between increased economic growth and achieving balance on current account
  - □ between increased economic growth and achieving equitable distribution of income

Resolving policy conflicts

- Policies that increase or decrease AD often lead to conflict.
  - □ Low inflation and balance on current account are helped by low AD.
  - □ Low unemployment and high economic growth are helped by high AD.
- Supply-side policies help resolve the conflict.
- Supply-side policies create conflict with achieving equitable distribution of income.

Do you know?

1 State the characteristics of both a positive and a negative output gap.
2 Outline the different causes of inflation.
3 Explain the difference between demand- and supply-side causes of unemployment.
4 Analyse why the Phillips curve is vertical in the long run.

2.4 Financial markets and monetary policy

You need to know

- what is meant by the money supply
- the main types and functions of the money markets
- how to calculate bond prices
- the different types of bank and their roles
- what monetary policy is and how it works
- how financial markets are regulated and the effects of regulation

Structure of financial markets and financial assets

Characteristics of money

- acceptable
- durable
- divisible
- portable
- scarce
- difficult to forge

Functions of money

Medium of exchange	Unit of account
Store of value	Standard of deferred payment

The money supply

Spectrum of liquidity				
Most liquid ◄──► Least liquid				
Notes and coins	**Bank current accounts**	**Bank savings accounts**	**Building society accounts**	**Other financial assets**
Approximately 2% of the UK money supply	Accessible through cash machines, cheques, debit cards, contactless payments, direct debits, standing orders and direct transfers	Usually instant access but access may be limited	Similar to banks but more often used for savings	Shares, bonds and bills, which can be converted into cash but not necessarily at face value

- There is no definitive definition of the money supply.
- There is a **spectrum of liquidity** (see the table above), ranging from very liquid assets (notes and coins) to less liquid items (e.g. physical assets, such as cars and property).
- A distinction is made between narrow money and broad money.

Narrow and broad money

Narrow money	Broad money
Notes and coins, current accounts Are immediately accessible	Includes narrow money but also other types of financial assets (bank and building society accounts) Not always immediately accessible Important measure of economic activity — e.g. shows willingness of households to borrow and spend money

Financial markets and their role in the wider economy

- Financial markets move money from people with a surplus (savers) to those with a shortage (borrowers).
- Financial markets enable:
  - □ individuals and firms to borrow
  - □ governments to finance budget deficits
  - □ international trade to occur
- There are three main financial markets:

Money market	Capital market	Foreign exchange market
Provides short-term finance to individuals, firms and governments Deals with very short-term loans (often repaid within hours, days, weeks or months) Covers interbank lending and **Treasury bills**	Deals with medium-to-long-term lending to firms and governments Deals mainly with issue, and trade, of bonds and shares Capital market is split into: - primary market — for issue of new securities (bonds and shares) - secondary market — trade in already issued bonds and shares (on 'stock markets')	Trade between different currencies Foreign exchange transactions are divided into: - spot market — immediate conversion between currencies - forward market — agreement to buy foreign currency at a specified later date

Key terms

Money supply The value of the stock of money in an economy.

Narrow money Notes and coins and other very liquid balances.

Broad money Narrow money plus balances held in financial institutions that may not be very liquid.

Money market Short-term finance provided for individuals, firms and governments.

Capital market Medium-to-long-term finance provided through bonds and equity.

Foreign exchange market Transactions in foreign currencies for immediate and future use.

Treasury bills Short-term debt borrowed by governments — usually repaid within three months.

The difference between equity and debt

Equity	Bonds (debt)
Equity is the share capital issued by firms	Bonds are issued by firms and governments wishing to borrow
Shares are sold to investors (shareholders) wishing to 'own' part of the business	Bonds pay a fixed rate of interest (the **coupon**) and have a fixed date of repayment (the **maturity date**)
Shares can be traded	Bonds have a range of lifespans (typically 10 years)
Investors buy shares to make capital gains and to receive dividends	Government bonds are also called **gilts**
Shareholders can vote at business meetings	Business bonds are often called **debentures**
Share prices rise and fall depending on investors' views on firm's future performance (in terms of profits)	

Relationship between market interest rates and bond prices

- Bonds are traded in the (secondary) capital market.
- Bond prices are closely connected with the level of current (market) interest rates.
- An inverse relationship exists between bond prices and current market interest rates.

Calculating the yield on bonds

- Bond yield is the interest paid on a bond as a percentage of the current price of a bond.
- The formula is:

$$\text{yield (\%)} = \frac{\text{coupon}}{\text{market price}} \times 100$$

For example, a bond with a coupon of 2% and a market price of £160 would have a yield of $2/160 \times 100 = 1.25\%$

- If interest rates rise, the price of already issued bonds falls (the coupon on those bonds — which is fixed — is now relatively lower than bonds now being issued).
For example, a bond valued at £100 with a 5% coupon would see its price rise to £200 if current interest rates fell to 2.5% (the price changes to match yields on new and existing bonds).

Commercial banks and investment banks

Commercial banks	Investment banks
Used by the public who open accounts with these	Not for the public to deposit funds
	Help businesses issue bonds and shares
Will lend to public as loans, overdrafts and mortgages	Assist governments with privatisations
	Trade in bonds, shares and foreign currencies to earn returns
	Act as brokers for investors looking to buy/sell bonds and shares

Functions of commercial banks

- Commercial banks move money from those with surpluses to those with shortages by:
  - ☐ accepting deposits from customers wishing to save
  - ☐ lending to individuals and businesses wishing to borrow
  - ☐ providing an efficient means of payment

Balance sheets of commercial banks

These are made up of:

Assets	Liabilities
Notes and coins	Share capital — finance raised to start up or to expand
Balances held at the Bank of England	
Money at call and short notice — held for short periods (e.g. overnight)	Reserves — profits reinvested into the bank
	Long-term borrowings — bonds issued by the bank to raise finance
Bills (commercial and Treasury) — short-term debts issued by businesses/governments	
	Short-term borrowings — amounts borrowed on the money markets to provide liquidity when the bank is short of money
Investments — shares and bonds issued by other companies/governments	
Advances — amounts lent to businesses and individuals	Deposits — amounts placed in the bank by customers
Tangible non-current assets — physical assets of the bank (e.g. bank premises)	

Objectives of commercial banks

- Banks aim to maximise profits to satisfy shareholders.
- Key objectives are divided into three areas:
  - ☐ liquidity — ensuring sufficient quantities of notes and coins to meet demand of customers
  - ☐ profitability — earning profits from lending money at a rate of interest

- □ security — managing the risk of lending money out to minimise the chances of debts not being collected
- ■ Liquidity and profitability are conflicting aims:
  - □ holding notes and coins improves liquidity
  - □ holding notes and coins is not a profitable activity
  - □ lending money generates profits but reduces liquidity

Credit creation

- ■ Bank customers are unlikely to withdraw all the money.
- ■ Banks only need to hold a small amount of the money deposited in liquid form (fractional banking).
- ■ Banks can create credit by lending money to customers wishing to borrow.
- ■ Money lent out to customers is (re)deposited in the banking system and then lent out again.
- ■ Credit creation is only limited by the amount banks wish to hold in liquid form.

Central banks and monetary policy

- ■ **Central banks** manage **monetary policy** for a country.
- ■ The UK's central bank is the Bank of England.
- ■ Its main functions are:
  - □ to maintain financial stability
  - □ to assist the government in maintaining macroeconomic stability

Financial stability

- ■ The Bank of England ensures financial stability by acting as a 'lender of last resort' — providing money for short-term needs to the banking sector if needed.
- ■ This helps ensure the banking system does not run out of money and fail.
- ■ This became very important during the 2008 financial crisis.

Macroeconomic stability

- ■ The main feature of monetary policy is the setting of interest rates (the **Bank rate**).
- ■ Other aspects of monetary policy include:
  - □ size of the money supply
  - □ availability of credit
  - □ exchange rate

> ### Key terms
>
> **Central bank** A bank responsible for a currency and managing monetary policy in an economy.
>
> **Monetary policy** Managing the price of money and the money supply for an economy.
>
> **Bank rate** The interest rate set by the Bank of England which influences all other interest rates in the economy.

- The Bank of England sets interest rates independently of UK government influence.
- Objectives of monetary policy include:
  - □ inflation target (measured by changes in CPI) of 2% per year ($\pm$ 1%).
  - □ achieving the inflation target through changes in the bank rate, decided by the Monetary Policy Committee (MPC)
  - □ full employment and steady economic growth

The Monetary Policy Committee

- The Monetary Policy Committee (MPC) consists of Bank of England employees and outside experts.
- When setting interest rates, the MPC considers factors affecting future inflation, such as:
  - □ consumer spending/confidence
  - □ business investment/confidence
  - □ fiscal stance (i.e. current tax rates and government spending)
  - □ exchange rate
  - □ commodity prices
  - □ house prices
  - □ labour market and wage rates
- Based on these factors, the MPC decides if interest rates need to change.
- There is a time lag between interest rate changes and changes in inflation of up to 2 years.
- Interest rate decisions are based on expectations of inflation up to 2 years in the future.
  - □ Expected increases in inflation mean interest rate rises are more likely.
  - □ Expected falls in inflation (or deflation) mean interest rate reductions are more likely.
- Interest rate changes significantly affect AD (and have minor effects on AS).

Interest rates and the exchange rate

- Changes in interest rates can affect the exchange rate:
  - □ Higher interest rates attract speculative flows of hot money.
  - □ Increased demand increases the currency's value (and vice versa).
- The link depends on expectations.
  - □ If interest rate changes are expected, then the exchange rate may not change when the interest rate changes.

The transmission mechanism of monetary policy

Figure 76 shows the **transmission mechanism** of a change in the Bank rate.

Key term

Transmission mechanism
The process of how a change in policy affects macroeconomic indicators and variables in the economy.

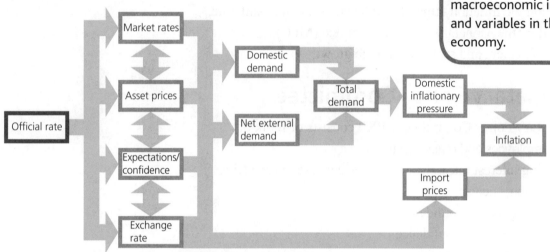

Figure 76 The monetary policy transmission mechanism

A rise in the Bank rate has the following effects:

- Interest rates charged by banks and other lenders will rise, which has the following effects on AD:
  - ☐ Consumers are more likely to save, and less likely to borrow and spend.
  - ☐ Households with mortgages are repaying more each month (assuming variable rate mortgages).
  - ☐ Business investment falls as the profitability of borrowing money to expand/invest will fall, given the higher cost of borrowing.
  - ☐ Asset prices are affected (bond prices will fall and this may also lead to falling share prices), which has a negative wealth effect on consumption.
  - ☐ The exchange rate will often rise, which leads to a fall in export volumes.
  - ☐ A rise in the exchange rate also leads to lower import prices — which increases imports.
- All these effects mean that AD falls from AD_1 to AD_2 in Figure 77.

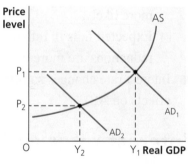

Figure 77 The effects of raising interest rates

Increasing interest rates also affects other economic objectives:

Lower economic growth (due to lower AD)	Higher unemployment (due to lower AD)
Improved current account balance (due to lower AD and less spent on imports)	Higher budget deficit (due to lower tax revenue and higher welfare expenditure)

Limitations of using interest rates

- time lags (up to 2 years for full effect of change)
- uncertainty over size of their impact
- difficult to use if interest rates already at low levels
- size of changes in interest rates may be difficult to decide
- conflict with other objectives

Bank of England and the money supply

- Interest rate changes affect the size of the money supply and the amount of credit in the economy.

Other ways the Bank of England can affect the money supply

> ### Key terms
>
> **Quantitative easing**
> Increasing liquid funds available for banks so that they are more willing to lend to businesses.
>
> **Forward guidance**
> Announcing the conditions for when policy is likely to change in the future.

Quantitative easing (QE)	Funding for lending scheme (FLS)	Forward guidance
Bank of England creates new money to buy bonds from financial institutions	Banks and lenders can swap assets (e.g. loans made) for Treasury bills — which are very liquid assets	Bank of England announces when policy changes are likely to occur, such as the likely date and size of future interest rate changes
This money can be lent out to create credit and increase AD	Treasury bills enable the banks and lenders to borrow money from other money markets at very low interest rates	Used less due to the UK economy behaving less predictably than expected (unemployment fell far sooner and lower than most economists expected)
QE was introduced in the UK in 2009 when banks were reluctant to lend even with very low interest rates	This encourages banks and lenders to borrow more and to lend out more in order to increase their profits	Forward guidance allows households and businesses to plan with greater confidence knowing when interest rates are likely to rise

Regulation of the financial system

UK financial regulation

- Until the 2008 financial crisis, regulation of the financial system was limited.
- Limited regulation was blamed for magnifying the financial crisis.
- The 2012 Financial Services Act introduced regulatory institutions designed to improve financial stability:

Prudential Regulation Authority (PRA)	Financial Conduct Authority (FCA)	Financial Policy Committee (FPC)
Responsible for supervision of banks and other financial institutions	Protects consumers by ensuring healthy competition between banks	Monitors, identifies and takes action to remove systematic risk from financial system
Takes actions to ensure these are managed properly and can make recommendations of action	Can intervene and set standards of behaviour if it feels institutions are not acting appropriately	Stress tests are conducted to see how 'healthy' banking sector is
Allows banks to fail if it doesn't disrupt whole financial system	Independent of the government	Concerned with macroprudential regulation, whereas PRA and FCA are concerned with microprudential regulation

Why banks fail and moral hazard

- Banks will face cash shortages if those it lends to fail to repay (by defaulting).
- If customers think the bank is short of cash, then a 'run' on the bank may occur.
- Runs on banks become self-fulfilling — the fear of banks running out of cash encourages more to withdraw their cash.
- The central bank can provide liquidity if the failure of a bank is against the public interest.
- Knowing a bank can be 'bailed out' creates a moral hazard and banks take too many risks, knowing they will not be allowed to fail.
- The 2012 Financial Services Act was designed to deal with the issue of moral hazard in the banking sector.

Liquidity and capital ratios

Liquidity ratios	Capital ratios
Limit bank lending by requiring banks to hold a percentage of their deposits in liquid form (i.e. as cash or as balances held at the Bank of England)	Place a limit on bank lending to a percentage of the bank's capital or equity issued
Increases in the liquidity ratio mean a bank can lend less — and cannot create as much credit	Should limit lending by banks compared with bank's own permanent capital
Should ensure banks have sufficient liquidity in case of a shortage	In 2019, a capital ratio (known as the liquidity coverage ratio) will be introduced for UK banks — capital must be equal to no less than 7% of their own lending

Systematic risk

- Financial crises often affect the whole banking sector (or spread from one bank to others).
- After a crisis, banks often become unwilling to lend.

Key terms

Moral hazard When an institution takes on too much risk due to not bearing the full costs of the risky behaviour.

Liquidity ratios Limiting how much lending a bank can make to a percentage of its deposits.

Capital ratios Limiting how much lending a bank can make to a percentage of its capital issued.

Systematic risk Risks that affect the whole banking system.

- Reduced bank lending has negative effects on the whole macroeconomy.
- Tighter regulation should reduce the chances of another crisis.

Issues with regulation

- Tighter controls restrict people/businesses from borrowing.
- Regulation may divert financial activities that contribute to GDP in other countries.
- Regulation requires time and money to plan, implement and monitor.
- Penalties are needed to deter excessive risk-taking.
- Unintended consequences are likely.

Synoptic link

Tighter regulation of banks may create an element of government failure — covered in Section 1.8.

Do you know?

1 What are the main functions of the different financial markets?
2 What are the differences between the two main different types of bank that exist?
3 How does an increase in interest rates affect macroeconomic indicators?
4 What are the main forms of financial regulation?

2.5 Fiscal policy and supply-side policies

You need to know

- the different types of tax used in the UK and their merits
- the reasons for and types of government spending
- the significance of the budget balance and the national debt
- the main types of supply-side policies and their application to the UK

Key terms

Fiscal policy Changes in government spending or taxation to achieve economic change.

Direct tax Taxes which cannot be avoided and are normally levied on incomes.

Indirect tax Taxes which can be passed on to others and are normally on expenditure.

Fiscal policy

Taxation

- Taxation finances government expenditure. Taxes fall into two main categories:
  - ☐ **direct taxes** — taxes on different forms of income
  - ☐ **indirect taxes** — taxes on expenditure

Synoptic link

Indirect taxes were covered in Section 1.8 on market failure.

Progressive, regressive and proportional taxes

Progressive taxes	Regressive taxes	Proportional taxes
Progressive taxes are paid in bands of income In the UK, 0%, 20%, 40% and 45% tax rates are used as incomes rise	Taxes on expenditure and fixed-sum taxes are often regressive if the expenditure is paid by all income earners in similar amounts VAT may be regressive if necessities are taxed	VAT may be proportional if only luxuries are taxed

UK's main taxes

- income tax — paid on income from employment
- national insurance contributions
- corporation tax
- capital gains tax
- inheritance tax
- value added tax (VAT)
- excise duties
- council tax
- stamp duty

Merits of different UK taxes

Taxes on incomes (e.g. income tax, corporation tax)	Taxes on expenditure (e.g. VAT)
Progressive tax may be equitable and alleviate relative poverty Income taxes create disincentives to work High income taxes encourage tax evasion/avoidance High business taxes may cause a 'brain drain' (or a failure to attract FDI)	Change patterns of expenditure (e.g. taxing demerit goods) Do not create disincentives to work/invest Possibly regressive Lead to underground/black markets

Why governments levy taxes

- Raise revenue to finance expenditure
- Change patterns of economic activity (e.g. taxes on demerit goods)
- Redistribute income (possibly via progressive taxes)
- Manage the macroeconomy (to change AD)
- Raise money for particular causes — hypothecated taxes

Principles of taxation

A good tax should be:

- economical
- equitable
- efficient
- convenient
- certain
- flexible

Key terms

Progressive tax A tax that increases as a proportion of income as income rises.

Regressive tax A tax that increases as a proportion of income as income falls.

Proportional tax A tax that is paid as an equal proportion of income at all levels of income.

Public (government) expenditure

Government spending is classed as either:

- current expenditure — spending on day-to-day costs in providing public services (e.g. NHS salaries)
- capital expenditure — spending on long-term projects (e.g. infrastructure)

Reasons for government expenditure

- provision of welfare
- provision of public goods
- provision of merit goods
- servicing the national debt
- macroeconomic management (affecting AD)
- supply-side improvements/ investment

Fiscal policy and aggregate demand

- Changes in tax and government spending affect AD.
- Changes in fiscal policy affect:
  - ☐ level of real GDP
  - ☐ unemployment rate
  - ☐ inflation rate

Expansionary fiscal policy	Contractionary fiscal policy
Fiscal policy that increases AD:	Fiscal policy that decreases AD:
■ higher government expenditure ■ lower rates of taxation	■ lower government expenditure ■ higher rates of taxation

- Changes in fiscal policy will affect AD via effects on consumption, investment and government expenditure.

Fiscal policy and aggregate supply

- Changes in fiscal policy also affect AS.
- Changes in indirect taxes affect SRAS (e.g. higher VAT shifts SRAS leftwards).
- Changes in government expenditure can affect LRAS (e.g. improvements to education).
- Changes in tax rates can encourage higher business investment in research, leading to supply-side improvements (LRAS).
- Fiscal policy can have microeconomic effects:
  - ☐ subsidies used to encourage consumption of certain goods
  - ☐ indirect taxes change patterns of behaviour

The budget balance

- The budget balance measures the difference between government spending and revenue from taxation.
  - ☐ budget deficit = government spending > taxation
  - ☐ budget surplus = government spending < taxation
- Budget balance measures a government's fiscal stance (how easy/ loose or tight/restrictive current policy is).
- Budget deficits are financed by the issue of bonds, adding to national debt.
- Budget surpluses allow the partial repayment of national debt.

> ### Key term
>
> **Budget balance** The difference between government spending and revenue from taxation.

Cyclical and structural budget deficits

A budget deficit can be caused by:

- expansionary fiscal policy
- low economic growth leading to low taxation revenue

Budget deficits can be analysed into two components — **cyclical budget deficits** and **structural budget deficits**.

Cyclical deficits	Structural deficits
Budget deficits resulting from lower than average economic growth	Budget deficits remaining when economic growth is average or above
When economic growth is lower than average, taxation revenue falls and government welfare spending increases	Faster economic growth reduces a budget deficit but the structural component remains
Cyclical deficits are eliminated by faster economic growth	Structural deficits are eliminated by reductions in government spending or increases in tax rates

Consequences of budget deficits and budget surplus

Economic growth	Unemployment	Inflation
Budget deficits add to AD and increase economic growth, whereas budget surpluses reduce AD and reduce economic growth Economic growth also affects the budget balance: - faster growth generates higher tax revenue and reduces a deficit - lower growth generates lower tax revenue and adds to a deficit	Expansionary fiscal policy increases a budget deficit and reduces unemployment Contractionary fiscal policy decreases a budget deficit and increases unemployment	Expansionary fiscal policy adds to AD and increases demand-pull inflation Contractionary fiscal policy reduces AD and decreases demand-pull inflation

Significance of the national debt

- **National debt** represents accumulated past budget deficits.
- Larger national debt means higher interest payments to service this debt (paid on each bond issued).
- If national debt becomes too large then investors buying bonds will demand higher interest rates on each bond issued — increasing government spending.
- National debt (as a percentage of GDP) falls if it grows at a slower rate than the rate of growth in GDP (economic growth).

Office for Budget Responsibility (OBR)

- OBR provides independent analysis of fiscal policy.
- It makes it harder for government to use fiscal policy for political motives.
- The main functions of OBR are:
  - □ economic forecasting
  - □ evaluating fiscal policy
  - □ analysis of public finances sustainability

Key terms

Cyclical budget deficit
A budget deficit caused by the effects of lower economic growth.

Structural budget deficit
A budget deficit which remains even when economic growth is average or higher.

National debt The accumulated stock of outstanding bonds issued, due for eventual repayment.

☐ evaluation of fiscal risks

☐ analysis of tax and welfare costing

Supply-side policies

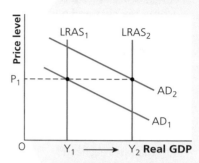

Figure 78 **Impact of successful supply-side policies**

- **Supply-side policies** (and **improvements**) allow increases in GDP without inflationary pressures emerging, shown in Figure 78 as LRAS increases from LRAS$_1$ to LRAS$_2$.

- Long-run economic growth is the result of improvements/increases in the supply side of the economy.

Economic effects of supply-side policies

Effects on GDP	Effects on unemployment	Effects on inflation	Effects on the current account of the balance of payments
Increasing the supply side of the economy should lead to higher GDP Long-run growth is increased with supply-side reform Actual growth can be increased through policies designed to increase (LR)AS and AD	Lower income taxes discourage people becoming voluntarily unemployed Reduced welfare benefits discourage voluntary and/or frictional unemployment Deregulation of markets (and privatisation) encourages competition, allowing businesses to expand — needing more workers Improvements in education should reduce occupational immobility and reduce structural unemployment Investment in infrastructure (especially transport) should reduce geographical immobility and reduce structural unemployment	Increase in LRAS means AD can be increased without demand-pull inflation emerging Trade union reform should reduce cost-push pressure (as wage increases are moderated) More competition in markets leads to less upward pressure on prices	Downward pressure on inflation should increase export competitiveness More productive workforce should mean exports are produced more cheaply Quality of output should improve, increasing demand for UK exports

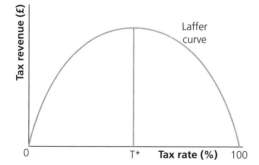

Figure 79 **The Laffer curve, showing how lower rates of tax can actually increase tax revenue**

Key terms

Supply-side policies Government policies to increase the productive capacity of the economy.

Supply-side improvements Natural increases in the productive capacity of the economy (e.g. higher birth rate).

Free market supply-side policies	Interventionist supply-side policies
Income tax cuts and personal incentives Cuts in income tax are a supply-side policy Lower income tax rates mean workers keep more of each £ earned This encourages more people to supply their labour and will increase the tax revenue earned as more people work This is shown on the Laffer curve diagram (see Figure 79); at tax rates above T*, cuts in tax will increase tax revenue until the rate reaches T*	**Education** Expansion of education and reform of education should increase LRAS in two ways: 1 Higher productivity of workers — due to future workers becoming more skilled in school or at college 2 Less structural unemployment as education can give the future workforce more transferable skills, allowing them to move between different jobs more easily
Reduction in trade union power Trade unions use collective strength to push wages above the free market equilibrium level Reducing trade union power makes it easier for firms to hire/fire workers	**Training** Increased training should boost productivity and improve the skills base of the workforce This can be provided directly by the government or by the private sector through subsidies/tax breaks
Reduction or elimination of the minimum wage Minimum wages create real-wage unemployment Reducing or abolishing minimum wages should move the wage rate back to its free market equilibrium level A minimum wage will add to or create real-wage unemployment — therefore reducing or abolishing the minimum wage reduces this type of unemployment	**Industrial policy** Government can encourage investment through grants, tax breaks and subsidies Other aspects of supply-side reform (labour market reform, educational reform) can also help industrial policy
Reduction in unemployment benefits Benefits make being unemployed more attractive and workers will take longer to move between jobs. Reducing the level of benefits or making it harder to qualify for benefits reduces voluntary and frictional unemployment.	**Research and development subsidies** Increased spending on R & D encourages technological advances and new innovations (all of which increases LRAS). This can be achieved through legislative changes as well as government spending and tax reform.
Reduction in labour protection Minimising or cancelling labour protection legislation reduces unemployment Firms are more willing to employ workers if the cost of employing workers is lower Employment is more likely if it is easier for firms to shed surplus labour Zero hours contracts are a good example of how firms can choose when to hire workers, but not pay for them when they are not needed Reductions in restrictions on working hours and making paternity and maternity leave less costly for businesses would also encourage them to recruit more workers	**Infrastructure investment** Governments spend money on infrastructure to improve economy's supply side Improvements to transport links (e.g. development of HS2) and improvements to digital communication make the economy function more efficiently (and may also reduce geographical immobility)
Privatisation and deregulation Transferring businesses from the public to the private sector (privatisation) should make businesses more efficient due to private businesses being more likely to pursue profits Privately owned businesses are more likely to cut costs and expand (and employ) than a public business Privatisation may be accompanied by deregulation to ensure actual competition Allowing private sector firms to compete with previously state-owned businesses should lead to lower prices and higher output (and higher quality as well) Private businesses are more likely to invest in new technology	**Entrepreneurship** Governments can encourage more people to create business start-ups through: ■ Provision of grants and other assistance for new start-ups ■ Improving enterprise education in schools and colleges ■ Removing barriers to setting up a business (this would be a free market supply-side policy)

Supply-side policies and fiscal policy

- Some supply-side policies can also be fiscal policy. These include:
  - ☐ tax changes
  - ☐ investment in education or infrastructure
  - ☐ provision of subsidies
- Other supply-side policies do not involve fiscal policy (e.g. deregulation, labour market reform).

Supply-side policies and the natural rate of unemployment

- The natural rate of unemployment (NRU) consists of voluntary, frictional and structural unemployment.
- The NRU can be reduced by supply-side policies, such as:
  - ☐ improvements to education to reduce factor immobility
  - ☐ incentives to increase training
  - ☐ investment in infrastructure
  - ☐ lower taxes on incomes
  - ☐ less generous welfare benefits
  - ☐ encouraging R & D

Limitations of supply-side policies

- Tax cuts often favour high earners.
- Welfare cuts fall disproportionately on lower income earners.
- Relative poverty is increased.
- There is a long time-lag with most policies.
- Investment in infrastructure is expensive and may be wasted.
- Workers' rights are reduced.

Key terms

Free market supply-side policies Policies to increase the productive capacity by making markets work more efficiently.

Interventionist supply-side policies Policies to increase the productive capacity by direct intervention in the macro economy (e.g. spending on infrastructure).

Synoptic link

The level of employment in an industry can also be studied using labour market analysis.

The policies of privatisation and deregulation are explored more thoroughly in Section 1.8.

Do you know?

1 Explain why indirect taxes have been increased to fund direct tax decreases.

2 Analyse the reasons why a government spends money in the economy.

3 Explain the link between a budget surplus and the national debt.

4 Explain how income tax reductions can both increase inflation but also decrease inflation.

5 Outline how higher government expenditure can improve the supply side of the economy.

2 National and international economy

2.6 The international economy

You need to know

- the causes and consequences of globalisation — including the effects of multinational corporations (MNCs)
- how trade affects a country's output
- how markets are protected and the case for protection
- what determines and affects the exchange rate
- the components of the balance of payments, its significance and how to correct deficits on the current account
- what development is and the causes of and barriers preventing it

Globalisation

Causes of globalisation	Main characteristics of globalisation
Improvements in communication (e.g. mobile phones and internet)	Greater foreign trade
Faster and cheaper transport (e.g. through containerisation)	Higher levels of overseas migration
Increased free trade	Increasing capital flows between countries
Closer political ties	Emergence of global brands
Abolition of capital controls	Greater use of outsourcing/offshoring

Key terms

Globalisation Increasing economic integration across international borders.

Free trade When two or more countries trade without barriers.

Consequences of globalisation

Consequences for more developed economies	Consequences for less developed economies
Potential for higher sales	Increased need to attract foreign direct investment (FDI)
Potential for economies of scale	Deciding whether to open local markets to businesses from developed economies
Increased competition from low-cost producers	Increased scrutiny of working conditions
Decline in manufacturing sectors	Adopting free market macroeconomic policies to attract capital
Increased use of outsourcing	

Exam tip

When thinking of the benefits of globalisation, always consider which perspective you are looking at them from.

108 | Need to know: AQA A-level economics

Role of MNCs

Benefits of MNCs to less developed economies	Drawbacks of MNCs to less developed economies
Employment boost	Wages offered by MNCs are often very low
Multiplier effects of FDI	
Wages may rise to attract local labour	MNCs may bring in their own workers
Tax revenue boosted	Tax avoidance by MNCs
Hard currency may be earned	Poor working conditions
	Environmental damage
	Increased competition for local businesses

Key terms

Multinational corporation (MNC) A business that operates in more than one country.

Absolute advantage One country being able to produce a product at a lower cost than in another country.

Trade

Foreign trade occurs because of:
- access to cheaper products
- greater variety of products
- lower production costs through specialisation and outsourcing

Model of comparative advantage

Absolute advantage

The example below illustrates **absolute advantage**, assuming:
- a two-country/two-product model
- that each country initially produces both products, with factors of production divided equally between production of food and clothing

	Food (output in units)	Clothing (output in units)
Country A	300	150
Country B	150	300
World total	450	450

- Country A has absolute advantage in food and country B in clothing — in each case, they can produce more than the other country.

- If each country were to specialise in its absolute advantage:

	Food (output in units)	Clothing (output in units)
Country A	600	0
Country B	0	600
World total	600	600

■ Specialisation increases world output.
■ Country A and country B can now trade, making each country better off than before.

Comparative advantage

In this instance, one country may be better at producing both products:

	Food (output in units)	Clothing (output in units)
Country A	400	800
Country B	200	50
World total	600	850

■ Country A has absolute advantage in both food and clothing.
■ Specialisation can still be beneficial if each country specialises in its comparative advantage.
■ **Comparative advantage** is measured by the opportunity cost of producing a product in terms of what could have been produced instead in the same country. So:
   - In country A: Opportunity cost of 1 unit of clothing is $\frac{1}{2}$ unit of food
   - In country B: Opportunity cost of 1 unit of clothing is 4 units of food
   □ Therefore, country A has comparative advantage in clothing.
   - In country A: Opportunity cost of 1 unit of food is 2 units clothing
   - In country B: Opportunity cost of 1 unit of food is $\frac{1}{4}$ unit of clothing.
   □ Therefore, country B has comparative advantage in food.

> ### Key term
>
> **Comparative advantage**
> One country being able to produce a product at a lower opportunity cost than another country.

If each country specialises in its comparative advantage, world output is as follows:

	Food (output in units)	Clothing (output in units)
Country A*	200	1200
Country B	400	0
World total	600	1200

(*) In this example, country A has partially specialised by putting quarter of its resources into food production and three quarters of resources into clothing production.

■ World output is higher than before specialisation.
■ Trade is mutually beneficial (at an appropriate exchange rate) — each country can consume more despite one country being less efficient at producing both products.

Assumptions of model

- factor immobility between countries
- perfect factor mobility within each country (e.g. workers can make either product)
- no economies or diseconomies of scale
- transport costs are small enough not to matter
- no artificial trade barriers

Changing pattern of UK trade

- The UK is an open economy — foreign trade accounts for around 30% of UK GDP.
- Trade with EU has grown over the last 50 years (though may decline once out of EU).
- There has been a gradual decline in trade with former Commonwealth countries.
- There has been a gradual decline in manufacturing exports.
- The UK has a high level of financial services exports.
- Areas of success for export include air technology, cars and military technology.

> ### Key term
>
> **Trade protection** Using artificial barriers known as protectionist policies to restrict the flow of imports into a country.

Protectionist policies

- Tariffs — taxes on imports.
  - ☐ Tariffs increase import prices, encouraging a switch to domestic alternatives — shown in Figure 80. As the world price rises from P_W to P_T, the quantity of imports falls from Q_1Q_2 to Q_3Q_4.
- Quotas — limits on the quantity of imports.
- Export subsidies — when governments subsidise export-producing industries.
- Red tape/artificial barriers — lengthy administrative procedures or complex legal standards for imports.

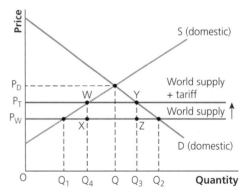

Figure 80 The effects of a tariff on imports

Arguments for protectionist policies	Arguments against/issues with protectionist policies
Protection of jobs	Based on comparative advantage, free trade maximises global output
Infant industry — protecting small domestic industries from larger, more efficient competition	Protecting infant/sunset industries encourages inefficiency
Anti-dumping — large overseas businesses selling output below cost to drive domestic businesses out	Higher prices (and possible job losses elsewhere due to reduced spending power)
Sunset industries — protecting industries in long-term decline	Protectionist policies usually encourage retaliatory measures
Strategic reasons — protecting strategically important industries (e.g. agriculture)	

Features of the single European market

- **Customs union**
- Freedom of movement of EU population
- Free movement of capital between members
- Common product standards and regulations
- Some fiscal coordination
- Some countries share monetary policy via Euro currency

Key terms

Customs unions Free trade areas with a common external tariff on imports from outside.

Balance of payments Record of financial transactions between UK and rest of the world.

BREXIT: the EU and the UK's decision to leave

Arguments in favour of leaving the EU	Arguments for remaining an EU member
Less competition from low-cost producers within EU	Larger market for UK businesses
Trade diversion — avoiding common external tariff on non-EU imports	Wider choice of products due to free trade access to single European market
No further financial contribution to EU (almost $10 billion per year)	Larger supply of skilled workers for UK business — often at lower wages
Less downward pressure on wages from EU migrants willing to work for low wages	Economies of scale
No need to comply with EU rules and regulations	Trade creation — access to tariff-free goods and services
UK unaffected by new laws made by European Parliament	

Role of the World Trade Organization

- More than 100 countries are World Trade Organization (WTO) members.
- WTO promotes trade liberalisation across membership.
- Trade negations are conducted in 'rounds'.
- WTO has been successful in reducing trade barriers (but progress has been very slow).
- Recent trend has been growth of regional trade blocks, such as EU, NAFTA and ASEAN.

Balance of payments

- The balance of payments consists of three sections:
  1 capital account
  2 financial account
  3 current account
- The balance on the total of the three sections affects the foreign currency holdings of the UK government:
  - ☐ A balance of payments deficit means foreign currency reserves fall.

- [ ] A balance of payments surplus means foreign currency reserves rise.
- A government can alternatively cover a balance of payments deficit by borrowing.
- If foreign reserves are insufficiently high to finance a current account deficit, then surplus must be generated on either the financial or capital account.

Capital account

- Contains some transfers and purchases/sales of non-financial assets.

Financial account

There are three components in the financial account:

- foreign direct investment (FDI) opening up/buying existing businesses located outside country of ownership
- portfolio investment — trade in financial assets (e.g. shares) outside country of ownership
- short-term movements of capital — into and out of a country, often moved for speculative motives and known as 'hot money'

Current account

Trade in goods	Trade in services	Primary income balance	Secondary income balance
Exports of goods – imports of goods	Exports of services – imports of services	Net investment income flows from interest, dividends and profits earned on overseas investments (less outflows from foreign-owned assets based in the UK)	Net transfers of money include: private transfers between countries (e.g. overseas workers sending wages back to home country), foreign aid, grants and gifts

Balance on current account

- Current account balance is measured by difference between inflows and outflows of money into and out of country due to:
  - [ ] exports and imports
  - [ ] investment income from factors of production located outside their country of ownership
  - [ ] transfers of money between countries
- Current account deficit: outflows > inflows
- Current account surplus: inflows > outflows
- UK current account is normally in deficit (surplus on services < deficit on goods).

Exam tip

Many news articles say 'balance of payments' when they really mean 'current account of the balance of payments'. As an economist, do not make the same mistake.

Factors determining exports	Factors determining imports
Foreign GDP — increases mean more demand for UK exports	UK GDP — increases mean more spending by UK consumers and more imports
Relative inflation	Relative inflation
Relative productivity	Relative productivity
Exchange rates — a higher exchange rate means exports appear more expensive overseas (and vice versa)	Exchange rates
	Both imports and exports are also affected by the level of trade barriers that exists

Policies to correct a deficit on the current account

- Achieving balance on current account is an economic objective.
- Deficits on current account can be corrected (eliminated or reduced) by:
  - □ expenditure-reducing policies — policies to reduce overall expenditure
  - □ expenditure-switching policies — policies to encourage a switch away from imports to exports.

Expenditure-reducing policy 1: deflation

- Reducing UK consumption leads to less imports.
- Reductions in UK consumption are achieved by:
  - □ higher interest rates
  - □ higher taxes
  - □ lower government spending

Issues with this policy:

- Unpopular with population.
- Conflicts with objectives for growth and unemployment.
- Higher interest rates may cause rise in exchange rate, which reduces exports.

Expenditure-switching policy 1: devaluation

- If currency falls (either by devaluation or by depreciation), then export prices appear cheaper overseas — so exports should rise.
- If currency falls then import prices rise — so imports should fall.

Issues with this policy:

Marshall–Lerner condition

- Devaluation *only* improves current account balance if Marshall–Lerner condition is satisfied.

> **Exam tip**
>
> Achieving balance on the current account will not always be high priority and often conflicts with achieving other, more important, objectives.

> **Key terms**
>
> **Expenditure-reducing policy** Reducing current account deficits through reductions in AD.
>
> **Expenditure-switching policy** Reducing current account deficits through encouraging switch away from imports to domestic output.

■ Marshall-Lerner condition:

> price elasticity of demand of exports + price elasticity of demand of imports > 1

■ If condition is not satisfied then devaluation will not improve current account balance at all.

The J curve

■ Devaluation will not immediately improve current account balance.
■ In the short run, demand for exports and imports is more price inelastic and demand for both doesn't change much.
■ However, imports now cost more, so value of imports rises — worsening current account balance.
■ In the medium term, demand for exports and imports becomes more price elastic — meaning demand for exports rises and demand for imports falls.
■ Current account balance eventually improves.
■ This gives us the J curve. Figure 81 illustrates that devaluation worsens deficit initially before it improves over time.

Expenditure-switching policy 2: protectionist policies

■ Creating trade barriers that prevent free trade.
■ Lead to lower levels of imports to improve the current account balance.
■ Methods used are covered earlier in this section.

Issues with this policy:
■ Protection usually leads to other countries retaliating, reducing UK exports.
■ Trade barriers are not allowed in some customs unions (e.g. EU).

Expenditure-switching policy 3: supply-side policies

■ Reforming an economy should lead to improvements in exports.
■ Improvements to productivity, infrastructure and education should boost exports' competitiveness.

Issues with this policy:
■ It takes many years to have a full effect.
■ It is difficult to measure.

Key term

J curve Observation that the current account balance will worsen before it improves following devaluation.

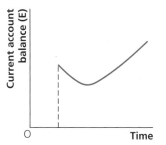

Figure 81 The J curve

Significance of deficits and surpluses

Achieving balance on current account is a government objective.

Reasons for wanting to avoid current account deficits	Reasons why current account deficits may not matter
A large current account deficit can indicate weaknesses in the export sector	Current account deficits may be due to high economic growth, which is more desirable
Interest rates may need to be higher to generate a surplus on the other parts of the balance of payments	A surplus on the financial account (e.g. from FDI) may 'cover' the current account deficit
Persistent deficits may lead to diminished foreign currency reserves (unless surplus exists on financial or capital accounts)	Deficits that are large when measured in £s may be small when measured as a % of GDP
If the government has insufficient foreign currency reserves, then it may need to borrow money or deflate the economy — i.e. reduce AD	This objective is usually seen as lower priority than achieving growth, employment and low inflation
Deficits often lead to falling currency values, which can boost cost-push inflation	

Implications of current account imbalances

- If governments attempt to eliminate a current account deficit, it will have knock-on effects across the world.
- A fall in spending on imports means a fall in exports from another country.
- Protectionist policies adopted by large economies can significantly affect the growth rate in smaller economies if they sell fewer exports to the larger economy.

Exchange rate systems

- Increases in the exchange rate (also known as strengthening, an appreciation or a revaluation) mean a currency buys more of another currency.
- Decreases in a currency are known as a weakening, a depreciation or a devaluation.
- Exchange rate systems can be either floating or fixed.

Floating exchange rate systems

- The exchange rate of floating currencies is determined by demand for and supply of the currency, as shown in Figure 82.

Synoptic link

The exchange rate is a price just like any other price. When the currency is floating, its price is determined by demand and supply.

Key terms

Exchange rate Price of one currency in terms of another currency.

Floating exchange rate Where currency can find its own free market level.

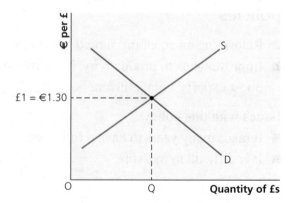

Figure 82 The exchange rate is determined by the demand for and supply of a currency

- A rise in demand for a currency leads to rising exchange rate (and vice versa), as shown by the shift from D_1 to D_2 in Figure 83.

- A rise in supply of a currency leads to falling exchange rate (and vice versa), as shown by the shift from S_1 to S_2 in Figure 84.

> **Exam tip**
>
> The pound (sterling) is freely floating and has been since 1992.

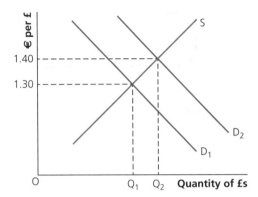

Figure 83 A rise in demand for the pound will lead to a rise in the exchange rate

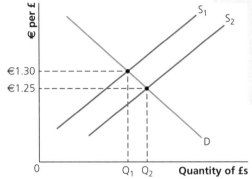

Figure 84 An increase in imports will increase the supply of pounds and lead to a fall in the exchange rate

Factors affecting a freely floating currency

Interest rates	Foreign trade	Relative inflation	FDI	Speculation/ expectations
Higher (relative) interest rates affect hot money flows Increases in interest rates lead to higher demand for a currency because of increases in hot money Higher demand for the currency leads to an exchange rate increase	Increased exports increase demand for the currency and subsequently the exchange rate Increased imports increase supply of a currency, leading to a fall in the exchange rate	If inflation is (relatively) higher then there will be a switch to relatively cheaper imports and a fall in exports Higher (relative) inflation will lead to a fall in the exchange rate	Higher FDI increases demand for the currency Higher FDI leads to a rise in the exchange rate	Exchange rates also change if there are expectations of a change in the determinants of a currency's value Speculators will buy a currency if they expect it to rise in the future (or sell if they think it will fall in the future)

Advantages and disadvantages of floating exchange rates

Advantages	Disadvantages
- Monetary sovereignty — ability to set interest rates for needs of domestic economy - No need to hold foreign reserves for currency stabilisation - Automatic adjustment to current account via exchange rate movements	- Business uncertainty over future value of currency - Currency may remain over/undervalued

> **Exam tip**
>
> Exchange rates don't always behave as expected by theory — the real world is far more complex, with many changes occurring simultaneously.

Fixed exchange rate systems

- Governments can fix the exchange rate by:
  - ☐ open market operations
  - ☐ monetary policy — interest rate changes
  - ☐ capital controls — restrictions on trade in currency

Advantages and disadvantages of fixed exchange rates

Advantages	Disadvantages
■ Easier for businesses to plan ■ No imported inflation ■ Monetary discipline — no politically motivated interest rate reductions	■ Loss of monetary sovereignty —stuck with inappropriate interest rate ■ Lack of adjustment available to restore price competitiveness of exports ■ Need to hold foreign currency reserves for foreign exchange market intervention

Currency unions

Arguments in favour of joining a currency union	Arguments against joining a currency union
■ Greater business certainty — encouraging intra-currency area trade ■ No conversion costs when exchanging currencies ■ Greater price transparency for consumers	■ Monetary policy set for whole currency area rather than for needs of individual economies ■ Business may not be able to compete with low-cost producers (and no exchange rate adjustment to help) ■ Fiscal policy needs to be used more actively ■ Countries may have to 'bail out' other members of currency zone

Economic growth and development

- Economic growth is measured by changes in national income.
- Development is multidimensional.
- Both are connected as growth feeds into development.
- Growth alone will not lead to development.

Characteristics of less-developed economies:
- low GDP per capita
- fast population growth
- primary product dependence
- poorly developed infrastructure and financial markets
- large informal economy
- large rural population/agricultural output

Indicators of development:

HDI is used by the United Nations and is a composite index, based on combined values for:

- real GDP per capita (PPP)
- health — based on life expectancy
- education — based on mean and expected years of schooling

Other measures of development:

- Human poverty index
- Gender-related development index (GDI)
- Gender empowerment measure (GEM)
- Social indicators

Factors affecting growth and development:

- Long-run growth comes from increases in LRAS or outward shifts in PPC.
- Development needs growth and improvements in:
  - ☐ investment in infrastructure — transport links, public services
  - ☐ education and training — boosting literacy rates and productivity of the workforce

Barriers to economic growth and development:

- Corruption
- Institutional factors
- Poor infrastructure
- Inadequate human capital
- Lack of property rights
- Lack of stable government
- Undeveloped financial system preventing businesses accessing funds
- Volatile earnings from exports (due to unstable commodity prices on which economy is over-reliant)

Policies to promote economic growth and development:

Market-based strategies	Interventionist strategies
Trade liberalisation — removal of trade barriers	Investment in infrastructure
Removal of subsidies	Investment in education and training
Policies to attract inward investment	Overseas aid
Allowing markets to work freely	Debt cancellation
	Welfare systems

Role of aid and trade in promoting growth and development:

Trade	Aid
Free trade helps development	Money, in the form of:
Free trade allows countries to benefit from their comparative advantage	■ soft loans — loans with conditions ■ unconditional transfers ■ goods and services, e.g. food, machinery etc.

Limitations of aid:
- Corruption may mean money only benefits small groups.
- Conditional aid may only benefit those granting the soft loans.
- Systems for using aid may not be in place (i.e. how it is shared out).
- Goods and services may be unsuitable.
- Money may be spent unwisely, even if motives are genuine.

Do you know?

1 Outline the arguments for and against a less developed country attracting FDI.
2 Explain the assumptions made within the model of comparative advantage.
3 Analyse the impact of devaluation on the current account of the balance of payments.
4 Show on a diagram the effects of a rise in interest rates on the exchange rate if the rise was unexpected.
5 Examine whether aid is good for less developed economies.

End of section 2 questions

Short questions

1 Define the term 'long-run aggregate supply'.
2 Define the term 'frictional unemployment'.
3 Define the term 'expansionary monetary policy'.
4 Define the term 'floating exchange rate'.

Longer questions

1 Analyse the impact of a cut in income tax on economic growth. (9 marks)
2 Analyse the consequences of high economic growth on an economy. (9 marks)
3 Analyse the methods taken by a government to reduce the natural rate of unemployment. (15 marks)
4 Analyse the factors that would lead to a fall in the value of a currency in a freely floating exchange rate. (15 marks).

Essay-style questions

1 To what extent is the GDP of an economy a good indicator of the living standards of its population? (25 marks)
2 To what extent do attempts to lower the unemployment rate conflict with a government's ability to achieve other macroeconomic objectives? (25 marks)
3 To what extent are current account deficits harmful for an economy? (25 marks)